15-MINUTE
SPANISH

D1448186

15-MINUTE
SPANISH
LEARN IN JUST 12 WEEKS

ANA BREMÓN

DK

London, New York, Munich, Melbourne, and Delhi

Senior Editor Angeles Gavira
Project Art Editor Vanessa Marr
DTP Designer John Goldsmid
Production Controller Luca Frassinetti
Publishing Manager Liz Wheeler
Managing Art Editor Philip Ormerod
Publishing Director Jonathan Metcalf
Art Director Bryn Walls

Language content produced for Dorling Kindersley by g-and-w publishing.

Produced for Dorling Kindersley by Schermuly Design Co.

First published in Great Britain in 2005 by
Dorling Kindersley Limited
80 Strand, London WC2R 0RL
Penguin Group (UK)

2 4 6 8 10 9 7 5 3 1
001–HD026–July/2012

A CIP catalogue record is available for this book
from the British Library.
ISBN 978-1-4093-7758-0

15-Minute Spanish is available as a book on its own,
in an audio pack with two CDs, or as part of a
complete language pack.

Printed and bound in China by Leo Paper Products LTD.

Discover more at
www.dk.com

CONTENTS

How to use this book

The main part of the book is devoted to 12 themed chapters, broken down into five 15-minute daily lessons, the last of which is a revision lesson. So, in just 12 weeks you will have completed the course. A concluding reference section contains a menu guide and English-to-Spanish and Spanish-to-English dictionaries.

Warm up
Each day starts with a one-minute warm up that encourages you to recall vocabulary or phrases you have learned previously. To the right of the heading bar you will see how long you need to spend on each exercise.

Instructions
Each exercise is numbered and introduced by instructions that explain what to do. In some cases additional information is given about the language point being covered.

Cultural/Conversational tip
These panels provide additional insights into life in Spain and language usage.

Text styles
Distinctive text styles differentiate Spanish and English, and the pronunciation guide (see right).

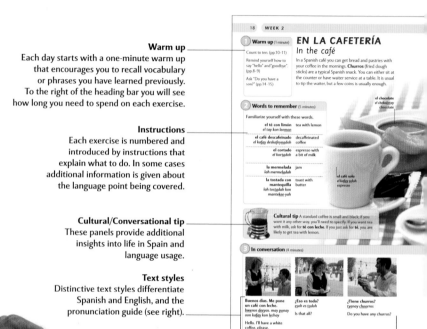

In conversation
Illustrated dialogues reflecting how vocabulary and phrases are used in everyday situations appear throughout the book.

How to use the flap
The book's cover flaps allow you to conceal the Spanish so that you can test whether you have remembered correctly.

Revision pages
A recap of selected elements of previous lessons helps to reinforce your knowledge.

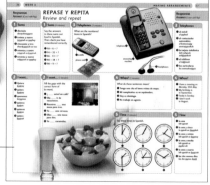

Pronunciation guide

This book teaches European Spanish, which differs in pronunciation from the various dialects spoken in Latin America. A few Spanish sounds require special explanation:

c   a Spanish **c** is pronounced *th* before **i** or **e** but **k** before other vowels: **cinco** <u>theen</u>koh (*five*)

h   **h** is always silent: **hola** o-lah (*hello*)

j (g)   a Spanish **j** (and **g** before **i** or **e**) is pronounced as a strong *h*, as if saying <u>h</u>at emphasizing the first letter

ll   pronounced *y* as in *yes*

ñ   pronounced *ny* like the sound in the middle of *canyon*

r   a Spanish **r** is trilled like a Scottish *r*, especially at the beginning of a word and when doubled

v   a Spanish **v** is halfway between an English *b* and *v*

z   a Spanish **z** is pronounced *th*

Spanish vowels tend to be pronounced shorter than their English equivalents:

a   as the English *father*
e   as the English *wet*
i   as the English *keep*
o   as the English *boat*
u   as the English *boot*

After each word or phrase you will find a pronunciation transcription, with underlining showing the stress. Remember that this can only be an approximation; there is no substitute for listening to and mimicking native speakers.

Useful phrases
Selected phrases relevant to the topic help you speak and understand.

Say it
In these exercises you are asked to apply what you have learned using different vocabulary.

Dictionary
A mini-dictionary provides ready reference from English to Spanish and Spanish to English for 2,500 words.

Menu guide
Use this guide as a reference for food terminology and popular Spanish dishes.

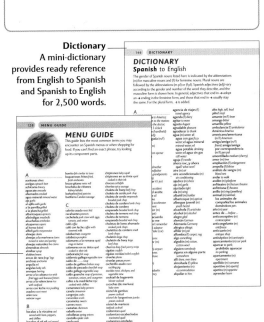

HOLA
Hello

In Spain women often greet with one or two kisses on the cheek and men shake other men's hands, although men may kiss or embrace younger male relatives or close friends. In more formal situations - among strangers or in a business context - a handshake is the norm.

¡Hola!
o-lah
Hello!

2 **Words to remember** (2 minutes)

Look at these greetings and say them aloud. Conceal the text on the left with the cover flap and try to remember the Spanish for each item. Check your answers.

Buenos días. *bwenos deeyas*	Good morning/ day.
Me llamo Ana. *may yamoh anna*	My name is Ana.
Encantado/-a. *enkan-tadoh/-ah*	Pleased to meet you (man/woman speaking).
Buenas tardes (noches). *bwenas tardes (noches)*	Good afternoon/ evening (night).

Cultural tip The Spanish frequently address people as **señor** (*sir*), **señora** (*madam*, for older women), and **señorita** (*miss*, for young women). With first names use **Don** for men or **Doña** for women: **Don Juan**, **Doña Ana**.

3 **In conversation: formal** (3 minutes)

Buenos días. Me llamo Concha García.
bwenos deeyas. may yamoh konchah garthee-ah

Good day. My name's Concha García.

Señor López, encantado.
senyor lopeth, enkan-tadoh

Mr López, pleased to meet you.

Encantada.
enkan-tadah

Pleased to meet you.

4 Put into practice (3 minutes)

Join in this conversation. Read the Spanish beside the pictures on the left and then follow the instructions to make your reply. Then test yourself by concealing the answers on the right with the cover flap.

Buenas tardes señor.	**Buenas tardes señora.**
bwenas tardes senyor	_bwenas tardes senyorah_

Good evening, sir.

Say: Good evening, madam.

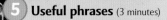

Me llamo Julia.	**Encantado.**
may yamoh hoolya	_enkan-tadoh_

My name is Julia.

Say: Pleased to meet you.

5 Useful phrases (3 minutes)

Read these phrases aloud several times and try to memorize them. Conceal the Spanish with the cover flap and test yourself.

What's your name?	**¿Cómo se llama?**
	komo seh yamah
Goodbye.	**Adiós.**
	addy-os
Thank you.	**Gracias.**
	grathyas
See you soon/tomorrow.	**Hasta pronto/mañana.**
	astah prontoh/manyanah

6 In conversation: informal (3 minutes)

Entonces, ¿hasta mañana?
entonthes, astah manyanah

So, see you tomorrow?

Sí, adiós.
see, addy-os

Yes, goodbye.

Adiós. Hasta pronto.
addy-os. astah prontoh

Goodbye. See you soon.

LAS RELACIONES
Relatives

1 Warm up (1 minute)

Say "hello" and "goodbye" in Spanish. (pp.8-9)

Now say "My name is...". (pp.8-9)

Say "sir" and "madam". (pp.8-9)

The Spanish equivalents of *mum* and *dad* are **mamá** and **papá**. The male plural can refer to both sexes, for example - **niños** (*boys* and *children*), **padres** (*fathers* and *parents*), **abuelos** (*grandfathers* and *grandparents*), **tíos** (*uncles* and *aunt* and *uncle*), **hermanos** (*brothers* and *siblings*), and so on.

2 Match and repeat (5 minutes)

Look at the people in this scene and match their numbers with the list at the side. Read the Spanish words aloud. Now, conceal the list with the cover flap and test yourself.

❶ **la hermana**
   lah air<u>ma</u>nah

❷ **el abuelo**
   el a<u>bwe</u>loh

❸ **el padre**
   el <u>pah</u>dray

❹ **el hermano**
   el air<u>ma</u>noh

❺ **la abuela**
   lah a<u>bwe</u>lah

❻ **la hija**
   lah <u>ee</u>-hah

❼ **la madre**
   lah <u>mah</u>dray

❽ **el hijo**
   el <u>ee</u>-hoh

grandfather ❷   ❸ father
sister ❶   ❹ brother
❺ grandmother   ❻ daughter   ❼ mother   ❽ son

Conversational tip In Spanish, things as well as people are masculine or feminine - for example, *wine* is masculine (**el vino**) but *milk* is feminine (**la leche**). Use **los** and **las** for masculine and feminine plurals, respectively. For *a/an*, use **un** for masculine and **una** for feminine items.

3 Words to remember: relatives (4 minutes)

el marido	**la mujer**
el mareedoh	*lah moo-hair*
husband	wife

Estoy casado/-a.
estoy kasadoh/-ah
I'm married (m/f).

Familiarize yourself with these words. Read them aloud several times and try to memorize them. Conceal the Spanish with the cover flap and test yourself.

father/mother-in-law	**el suegro/la suegra**
	el swegroh/lah swegrah
stepfather	**el padrastro**
	el padras-troh
stepmother	**la madrastra**
	lah madras-trah
children (male/female)	**los niños/las niñas**
	los neenyos/las neenyas
uncle/aunt	**el tío/la tía**
	el tee-oh/ lah tee-ah
cousin	**el primo/la prima**
	el preemoh/lah preemah
I have four children.	**Tengo cuatro niños.**
	tengoh kwatroh neenyos
I have two stepdaughters and a stepson.	**Tengo dos hijastras y un hijastro.**
	tengoh dos ee-hastras ee oon ee-hastroh

4 Words to remember: numbers (3 minutes)

Memorize these words and then test yourself using the cover flap.

Careful when you use the number *one*. When you use **uno** in front of a word it changes to **un** or **una**, depending on whether that word is masculine or feminine. For example: **Tengo un hijo** (*I have one son*), **Tengo una hija** (*I have one daughter*).

one	**uno/-a**
	oonoh/-ah
two	**dos**
	dos
three	**tres**
	tres
four	**cuatro**
	kwatroh
five	**cinco**
	theenkoh
six	**seis**
	seys
seven	**siete**
	syetay
eight	**ocho**
	ochoh
nine	**nueve**
	nwebay
ten	**diez**
	dyeth

5 Say it (2 minute)

I have five sons.

I have three sisters and a brother.

I have two children.

MI FAMILIA
My family

1 Warm up (1 minute)

Say the Spanish for as many members of the family as you can. (pp.10-11)

Say "I have two sons". (pp.10-11)

There are two ways of saying *you* in Spanish, **usted** for formal situations and **tú** in informal ones. There is also a formal way of saying *your* - **su** (singular) and **sus** (plural): **usted y su mujer** (*you and your wife*), **¿Son ésos sus hijos?** (*Are those your sons?*). **Su** and **sus** also mean *his* and *her*.

2 Words to remember (5 minutes)

Say these words aloud a few times. Conceal the Spanish with the cover flap and try to remember the Spanish word for each item.

mi *mee*	my (with singular)
mis *mees*	my (with plural)
tu *too*	your (informal with singular)
tus *toos*	your (informal with plural)
su *soo*	your (formal with singular)
sus *soos*	your (formal with plural)
su *soo*	his/her (with singular) their (with singular)
sus *soos*	his/her (with plural) their (with plural)

Éstos son mis padres.
estos son mees pahdres
These are my parents.

3 In conversation (4 minutes)

¿Tiene usted niños?
tyenay oosted neenyos

Do you have any children?

Sí, tengo dos hijas.
see, tengoh dos ee-has

Yes, I have two daughters.

Éstas son mis hijas. ¿Y usted?
estas son mees ee-has. ee oosted

These are my daughters. And you?

Conversational tip The Spanish ask a question by simply raising the pitch of the voice at the end of a statement: **¿Quieres un poco de vino?** (*Do you want a little wine?*). Notice the upside-down question mark (**¿**) written at the beginning of the question. You will also see an upside-down exclamation mark, as in **¡Hola!** (*Hello!*).

4 Useful phrases (3 minutes)

Read these phrases aloud several times and try to memorize them. Conceal the Spanish with the cover flap and test yourself.

Do you have any brothers? (formal)	**¿Tiene usted hermanos?** *tyenay oosted airmanos*
Do you have any brothers? (informal)	**¿Tienes hermanos?** *tyenes airmanos*

This is my husband.	**Éste es mi marido.** *estay es mee mareedoh*
That's my wife.	**Ésa es mi mujer.** *esah es mee moo-hair*

Is that your sister? (formal)	**¿Es ésa su hermana?** *es esah soo airmanah*
Is that your sister? (informal)	**¿Es ésa tu hermana?** *es esah too airmanah*

5 Say it (2 minutes)

Do you have any brothers and sisters? (formal)

Do you have any children? (informal)

I have two sisters.

This is my wife, María.

No, pero tengo un hijastro.
noh, peroh tengoh oon ee-hastroh

No, but I have a stepson.

1 **Warm up** (1 minute)

Say "See you soon".
(pp.8-9)

Say "I am married"
(pp.10-11) and "I have
a wife". (pp.12-13)

SER Y TENER
To be and to have

Two of the most important verbs are **ser** (to be)
and **tener** (to have). Note that there are different
ways of saying *you*, *we*, and *they*, with formal and
informal, singular and plural, and masculine
and feminine forms. Pronouns (*I*, *you*, etc.) are
omitted where the sense is clear.

2 **Ser: to be** (5 minutes)

Familiarize yourself with **ser** (to be). When you are
confident, practise the sample sentences below.
Note: there is another verb meaning "to be" -
estar, which is discussed on page 49.

yo soy *yoh soy*	I am
tú eres *too eh-res*	you are (informal singular)
usted es *oosted es*	you are (formal singular)
él/ella es *el/eh-yah es*	he/she is
nosotros/-as somos *nosotros/-as somos*	we are (masculine/ feminine)
vosotros/-as sois *bosotros/-as soys*	you are (informal plural, m/f)
ustedes son *oostedes son*	you are (formal plural)
ellos/-as son *eh-yos/-yas son*	they are (masculine/ feminine)

Yo soy inglesa.
yoh soy eenglesah
I'm English.

¿De dónde es usted? *day donday es oosted*	Where are you from?
Es mi hermana. *es mee airmanah*	She is my sister.
Somos españoles. *somos espanyoles*	We're Spanish.

3 Tener: to have (5 minutes)

Practise **tener** (to have) and the sample sentences, then test yourself.

I have	**yo tengo** *yoh tengoh*
you have (informal singular)	**tú tienes** *too tyenes*
you have (formal singular)	**usted tiene** *oosted tyenay*
he/she has	**él/ella tiene** *el/eh-yah tyenay*
we have (masculine/feminine)	**nosotros/-as tenemos** *nosotros/-as tenaymos*
you have (informal plural, m/f)	**vosotros/-as teneis** *bosotros/-as tenays*
you have (formal plural)	**ustedes tienen** *oostedes tyenen*
they have (masculine/feminine)	**ellos/-as tienen** *eh-yos/-yas tyenen*

¿Tiene rosas rojas?
 tyenay rosas rohas
 Do you have red roses?

He has a meeting.	**Tiene una reunión.** *tyenay oonah re-oonyon*
Do you have a mobile phone?	**¿Tiene usted móvil?** *tyenay oosted mobeel?*
How many brothers and sisters do you have?	**¿Cuántos hermanos tiene usted?** *kwantos airmanos tyenay oosted*

4 Negatives (4 minutes)

la bicicleta
 lah beetheekletah
 bicycle

No tengo coche.
 noh tengoh kochay
 I don't have a car.

It is easy to make sentences negative in Spanish, just put **no** in front of the verb: **No somos americanos** (We're not American).

I'm not Spanish.	**No soy español.** *noh soy espanyol*
He's not a vegetarian.	**No es vegetariano.** *noh es be-hetaryanoh*
We don't have any children.	**No tenemos niños.** *noh tenaymos neenyos*

REPASE Y REPITA
Review and repeat

Respuestas
Answers (Cover with flap)

1 How many

❶ tres
tres

❷ nueve
nwebay

❸ cuatro
kwatroh

❹ dos
dos

❺ ocho
ochoh

❻ diez
dyeth

❼ cinco
theenkoh

❽ siete
syetay

❾ seis
seys

1 How many (2 minutes)

Cover the answers with the flap. Then say these Spanish numbers out loud. Check you have remembered the Spanish correctly.

3 ❶
9 ❷
4 ❸
2 ❹
8 ❺
10 ❻
5 ❼
7 ❽
6 ❾

2 Hello

❶ Buenos días. Me llamo... [your name].
bwenos deeyas. may yamoh...

❷ Encantado/-a.
enkan-tadoh/-ah

❸ Sí, y tengo dos hijos. ¿Y usted?
see, ee tengoh dos ee-hos. ee oosted

❹ Adiós. Hasta mañana.
addy-os. astah manyanah

2 Hello (4 minutes)

You are talking to someone you have just met. Join in the conversation, replying in Spanish following the English prompts.

Buenos días. Me llamo María.
❶ Answer the greeting and give your name.

Éste es mi marido, Juan.
❷ Say "Pleased to meet you".

¿Está usted casado/-a?
❸ Say "Yes, and I have two sons. And you?"

Nosotros tenemos tres hijos.
❹ Say "Goodbye. See you tomorrow".

3 To have or be (5 minutes)

Fill in the blanks with the correct form of **tener**
(*to have*) or **ser** (*to be*). Check you have remembered
the Spanish correctly.

1 Yo _____ inglesa.

2 Nosotros _____ cuatro niños.

3 Yo no _____ feliz.

4 ¿ _____ tú coche?

5 Él _____ mi marido.

6 Yo no _____ teléfono móvil.

7 Tú no _____ español.

8 ¿ _____ usted hijos?

3 To have or be

1 soy
   soy

2 tenemos
   tenaymos

3 soy
   soy

4 tienes
   tyenes

5 es
   es

6 tengo
   tengoh

7 eres
   eh-res

8 tiene
   tyenay

4 Family (4 minutes)

Say the Spanish for each of the numbered family
members. Check you have remembered the
Spanish correctly.

grandfather **2**   **3** father
sister **1**   **4** brother

6 daughter
5 grandmother   **7** mother   **8** son

4 Family

1 la hermana
   lah airmanah

2 el abuelo
   el abweloh

3 el padre
   el pahdray

4 el hermano
   el airmanoh

5 la abuela
   lah abwelah

6 la hija
   lah ee-ha

7 la madre
   lah mahdray

8 el hijo
   el ee-hoh

EN LA CAFETERÍA
In the café

1 **Warm up** (1 minute)

Count to ten. (pp.10-11)

Remind yourself how to say "hello" and "goodbye". (pp.8-9)

Ask "Do you have a son?" (pp.14-15)

In a Spanish café you can get bread and pastries with your coffee in the mornings. **Churros** (fried dough sticks) are a typical Spanish snack. You can either sit at the counter or have waiter service at a table. It is usual to tip the waiter, but a few coins is usually enough.

el chocolate
el chokolatay
chocolate

2 **Words to remember** (5 minutes)

Familiarize yourself with these words.

el té con limón *el tay kon leemon*	tea with lemon
el café descafeinado *el kafay deskafeynadoh*	decaffeinated coffee
el cortado *el kortadoh*	espresso with a bit of milk
la mermelada *lah mermeladah*	jam
la tostada con mantequilla *lah tostadah kon mantekee-yah*	toast with butter

el café solo
el kafay soloh
espresso

Cultural tip A standard coffee is small and black; if you want it any other way, you'll need to specify. If you want tea with milk, ask for **té con leche**. If you just ask for **té**, you are likely to get tea with lemon.

3 **In conversation** (4 minutes)

Buenos días. Me pone un café con leche.
bwenos deeyas. may ponay oon kafay kon lechay

Hello. I'll have a white coffee, please.

¿Eso es todo?
esoh es todoh

Is that all?

¿Tiene churros?
tyenay choorros

Do you have any churros?

4 Useful phrases (5 minutes)

Learn these phrases. Read the English under the pictures and say the phrase in Spanish as shown on the right. Then cover the Spanish with the cover flap and test yourself.

los churros
los choorros
churros

el azúcar
el ah-thookar
sugar

el café con leche
el kafay kon lechay
white coffee

I'll have a black coffee.

Me pone un café.
may ponay oon kafay

Is that all?

¿Eso es todo?
esoh es todoh

I'm going to have some churros.

Yo voy a tomar churros.
yoh boy ah tomar choorros

How much is that?

¿Cuánto es?
kwantoh es

Sí, señor.
see, senyor

Yes, sir.

Gracias. ¿Cuánto es?
grathyas. kwantoh es

Thank you. How much is that?

Cuatro euros, por favor.
kwatroh eh-ooros, por fabor

Four euros, please.

Warm up (1 minute)

Ask "How much is that?"
(pp.18-19)

Say "I don't have a
brother". (pp.14-15)

Ask "Do you have any
churros?" (pp.18-19)

EN EL RESTAURANTE
In the restaurant

There are a variety of different types of eating places
in Spain. In a bar or **tasca** you can find a few **tapas** or
snacks. Lunch is the main meal of the day, but if you are
not very hungry, many restaurants offer **tapas** at the
bar, which is usually very good value for a light meal.

Words to remember (3 minutes)

Memorize these words. Conceal
the Spanish with the cover flap
and test yourself.

la carta *lah kartah*	menu
la carta de vinos *lah kartah day beenos*	wine list
los entrantes *los entrantes*	starters
el plato principal *el platoh preentheepal*	main course
los postres *los postres*	desserts
el desayuno *el desah-yoonoh*	breakfast
el almuerzo *el almooairthoh*	lunch
la cena *lah thenah*	dinner

cup ❼

saucer ❽

❺ spoon

❻ knife

fork ❹

In conversation (4 minutes)

**Hola. Una mesa para
cuatro, por favor.**
*o-lah. oonah mesah parah
kwatroh, por fabor*

Hello. A table for
four, please.

¿Tiene una reserva?
tyenay oonah reserbah

Do you have a reservation?

Sí, a nombre de Cortés.
see, ah nombray day kortes

Yes, in the name of Cortés.

4 Match and repeat (4 minutes)

Look at the numbered objects on this table and match them with the items in the vocabulary list at the side. Read the Spanish words aloud. Now, conceal the list with the cover flap and test yourself.

glass ❶

❷ napkin

plate ❸

❶ **la copa**
lah kopah

❷ **la servilleta**
lah serbee-yetah

❸ **el plato**
el platoh

❹ **el tenedor**
el tenedor

❺ **la cuchara**
lah koocharah

❻ **el cuchillo**
el koochee-yoh

❼ **la taza**
lah tathah

❽ **el platillo**
el plateeyoh

5 Useful phrases (4 minutes)

Learn these phrases and then test yourself using the cover flap to conceal the Spanish.

What do you have for dessert?	**¿Qué tiene de postre?** *kay tyenay day postray*
The bill, please.	**La cuenta, por favor.** *lah kwentah, por fabor*

¿Fumadores o no fumadores?
foomadores oh noh foomadores

Smoking or non-smoking?

No fumadores, por favor.
noh foomadores, por fabor

Non-smoking, please.

Síganme, por favor.
seegan-may, por fabor.

Follow me, please.

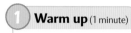

QUERER
To want

① Warm up (1 minute)

What are "breakfast", "lunch", and "dinner" in Spanish? (pp.20-1)

Say "I", "you" (informal), "he", "she", "we", "you" (plural/formal), "they" (masculine), "they" (feminine). (pp.14-15)

Querer (*to want*) is a verb that is essential to everyday conversation. There is also a polite form, **quisiera** (*I'd like*). Use this when requesting something because quiero (*I want*) may sound too strong: **¿Qué quiere beber?** (*What do you want to drink?*); **Quisiera una cerveza** (*I'd like a beer*).

② Querer: to want (6 minutes)

Say the different forms of **querer** (*to want*) aloud. Use the cover flap to test yourself and, when you are confident, practise the sample sentences below.

yo quiero *yoh kyairoh*	I want
tú quieres/usted quiere *too kyaires/oosted kyairay*	you want (singular, informal/formal)
él/ella quiere *el/eh-yah kyairay*	he/she wants
nosotros/-as queremos *nosotros/-as keraymos*	we want (masculine/feminine)
vosotros/-as queréis/ ustedes quieren *bosotros/-as kerays/ oostedes kyairen*	you want (plural, informal/formal)
ellos/-as quieren *eh-yos/-as-yas kyairen*	they want (masculine/feminine)
¿Quieres vino? *kyaires beenoh?*	Do you want some wine?
Quiere un coche nuevo. *kyairay oon kochay nweboh*	She wants a new car.

Quiero caramelos.
kyairoh karamelos
I want some sweets.

Conversational tip Although it may sound rude to you, Spaniards don't say *please* (**por favor**) or *thank you* (**gracias**) very often, and they hardly ever say *excuse me* (**perdón**) or *I'm sorry* (**lo siento**), but they use the tone of their voices and choice of words to imply politeness, such as **quisiera** (*I'd like*) instead of **quiero** (*I want*).

3 Polite requests (4 minutes)

Practise the following sample phrases that use
quisiera (*I'd like*), the form of **quiero** (*I want*)
that is used for polite requests.

I'd like a beer.	**Quisiera un cerveza.**
	keesyairah oon
	therbaythah

I'd like a table for tonight.	**Quisiera una mesa para esta noche.**
	keesyairah oonah mesah parah estah nocheh

I'd like to see the menu, please.	**Quisiera ver la carta, por favor.**
	keesyairah ber lah kartah, por fabor

4 Put into practice (4 minutes)

Join in this conversation. Read the Spanish beside
the pictures on the left and follow the instructions
to make your reply. Then test yourself by concealing
the answers using the cover flap.

Buenas tardes señor. ¿Tiene una reserva? *bwenas tardes senyor. tyeneh oonah reserbah*	**No, pero quisiera una mesa para tres.** *noh, peroh keesyairah oonah mesah parah tres*

Good evening, sir. Do you have a reservation?

Say: No, but I would like a table for three.

Muy bien. ¿Qué mesa le gustaría? *mwee byen. kay mesah le goostareeyah*	**Cerca de la ventana, por favor.** *therkah day lah bentanah, por fabor*

Very good. Which table would you like?

Say: Near the window please.

LOS PLATOS
Dishes

Warm up (1 minute)

Say "She's happy" and
"I'm not sure". (pp.14-15)

Ask "Do you have
churros?" (pp.18-19)

Say "I'd like a white
coffee". (pp.18-19)

Spain offers a large variety of regional dishes. Plenty of
garlic and olive oil are a feature of many typical dishes.
Not many restaurants offer a vegetarian menu, but
there are, however, many traditional Spanish dishes
that do not contain meat. Ask your waiter for advice.

Cultural tip At lunch time, you will find that many
restaurants offer **el menú del día** (*the day's set menu*).
This is usually a three-course meal, with bread and
drink included in the price.

Match and repeat (4 minutes)

Match the numbered items to
the Spanish words in the panel.

❶ **las verduras**
las ber<u>doo</u>ras

❷ **la fruta**
lah <u>froo</u>tah

❸ **el queso**
el <u>kes</u>oh

❹ **los frutos secos**
los <u>froo</u>tos <u>se</u>kos

❺ **la sopa**
lah <u>so</u>pah

❻ **las aves**
las <u>ah</u>bes

❼ **el pescado**
el pes<u>ka</u>doh

❽ **la pasta**
lah <u>pas</u>tah

❾ **el marisco**
el ma<u>rees</u>koh

❿ **la carne**
lah <u>kar</u>nay

fruit ❷

vegetables ❶

cheese ❸

❺ soup

poultry ❻

❽ pasta

❾ seafood

3 Words to remember: cooking methods (3 minutes)

The ending often varies depending on the gender of item described.

fried (m/f)	**frito/-a** _free_toh/-ah
grilled	**a la plancha** ah lah _plan_chah
roasted (m/f)	**asado/-a** ah_sa_doh/-ah
boiled (m/f)	**hervido/-a** er_bee_doh/-ah
steamed	**al vapor** al ba_por_
rare (m/f)	**poco hecho/-a** pokoh _eh_-choh/-ah

Quisiera mi filete bien hecho.
_kees_yairah mee _feele_tay byen _eh_-choh
I'd like my steak well done.

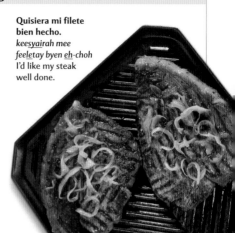

6 Say it (2 minutes)

What is **tortilla**?

I'm allergic to seafood.

I'd like a beer.

nuts ④

fish ⑦

⑩ meat

4 Words to remember: drinks (3 minutes)

Familiarize yourself with these words.

water	**el agua** el _ah_gwah
fizzy water	**el agua con gas** el _ah_gwah kon gas
still water	**el agua sin gas** el _ah_gwah seen gas
wine	**el vino** el _bee_noh
beer	**la cerveza** lah thair_bay_thah
fruit juice	**el zumo** el _thoo_moh

5 Useful phrases (2 minutes)

Learn these phrases and then test yourself.

I am a vegetarian. (m/f)	**Soy vegetariano/-a.** soy be-hetar_eea_noh/-ah
I am allergic to nuts. (m/f)	**Soy alérgico/-a a los frutos secos.** soy ahl_er_-heekoh/-ah ah los _froo_tos _se_kos
What is "conejo"?	**¿Qué es "conejo"?** kay es ko_ne_-hoh

REPASE Y REPITA
Review and repeat

Respuestas
Answers (Cover with flap)

① What food?

❶ los frutos secos
los frootos sekos

❷ el marisco
el mareeskoh

❸ la carne
lah karnay

❹ el azúcar
el ah-thookar

❺ la copa
lah kopah

① What food? (4 minutes)

Name the numbered items.

❶ nuts
sugar ❹
seafood ❷
meat ❸
glass ❺

② This is my...

❶ Ésta es mi mujer.
estah es mee moo-hair

❷ Aquí están sus hijas.
ahkee estan soos ee-has

❸ Su mesa es de no fumadores.
soo mesah es day noh foomadores

② This is my... (4 minutes)

Say these phrases in Spanish. Use **mi(-s)**, **tu(-us)** or **su(-s)**.

❶ This is my wife.
❷ Here are her daughters.
❸ Their table is non-smoking.

③ I'd like...

❶ Quisiera un café.
keesyairah oon kafay

❷ Quisiera churros.
keesyairah choorros

❸ Quisiera azúcar.
keesyairah ah-thookar

❹ Quisiera un café con leche.
keesyairah oon kafay kon lechay

③ I'd like... (3 minutes)

Say "I'd like" the following:

❶ black coffee
churros ❷
❸ sugar
white coffee ❹

6 pasta

knife 7

8 cheese

beer 10

9 napkin

1 What food?

6 **la pasta**
lah pastah

7 **el cuchillo**
el koochee-yoh

8 **el queso**
el kesoh

9 **la servilleta**
lah serbee-yetah

10 **la cerveza**
lah thairbaythah

4 Restaurant (4 minutes)

You arrive at a restaurant. Join in the conversation, replying in Spanish following the English prompts.

Buenas tardes señora, señor.
1 Ask for a table for six.

¿Fumadores o no fumadores?
2 Say: non-smoking.

Síganme, por favor.
3 Ask for the menu.

¿Quiere la carta de vinos?
4 Say: No. Fizzy water, please.

Muy bien.
5 Say you don't have a glass.

4 Restaurant

1 **Buenas tardes, quisiera una mesa para seis.**
bwenas tardes, keesyairah oonah mesah parah seys

2 **No fumadores.**
noh foomadores

3 **La carta, por favor.**
lah kartah, por fabor

4 **No. Agua con gas, por favor.**
noh. ahgwah kon gas, por fabor

5 **No tengo copa.**
noh tengoh kopah

LOS DÍAS Y LOS MESES
Days and months

1 **Warm up** (1 minute)

Say "he is" and "they are". (pp.14–15)

Say "he is not" and "they are not". (pp.14–15)

What is Spanish for "the children"? (pp.10–11)

In Spanish, *days of the week* (**los días de la semana**) and *months* (**los meses**) do not have capital letters Notice that you use **en** with months: **en abril** (*in April*), but **el** or **los** with days: **el/los lunes** (*on Monday/Mondays*).

2 **Words to remember: days of the week** (5 minutes)

Familiarize yourself with these words and test yourself using the cover flap.

lunes *loones*	Monday
martes *martes*	Tuesday
miércoles *myairkoles*	Wednesday
jueves *hwebes*	Thursday
viernes *byernes*	Friday
sábado *sabadoh*	Saturday
domingo *domeengoh*	Sunday
hoy *oy*	today
mañana *manyanah*	tomorrow
ayer *ah-yair*	yesterday

Nos reunimos mañana.
mos reh-ooneemos manyanah
We meet tomorrow.

Tengo una reserva para hoy.
tengoh oonah reserbah parah oy
I have a reservation for today.

3 **Useful phrases: days** (2 minutes)

Learn these phrases and then test yourself using the cover flap.

La reunión no es el martes. *lah reh-oonyon noh es el martes*	The meeting isn't on Tuesday.
Trabajo los domingos. *traba-hoh los domeengos*	I work on Sundays.

4 Words to remember: months (5 minutes)

Familiarize yourself with these words and test yourself using the cover flap.

Nuestro aniversario es en julio.
nwestroh aneebairsaree-oh es en hoolee-oh
Our anniversary is in July.

Navidad es en diciembre.
nabeedad es en deethyembray
Christmas is in December.

January	**enero**
	ehneroh
February	**febrero**
	febreroh
March	**marzo**
	marthoh
April	**abril**
	abreel
May	**mayo**
	mah-yoh
June	**junio**
	hoonee-oh
July	**julio**
	hoolee-oh
August	**agosto**
	agostoh
September	**septiembre**
	septyembray
October	**octubre**
	oktoobray
November	**noviembre**
	nobyembray
December	**diciembre**
	deethyembray
month	**el mes**
	el mes
year	**el año**
	el anyoh

5 Useful phrases: months (2 minutes)

Learn these phrases and then test yourself using the cover flap.

My children are on holiday in August.	**Mis hijos están de vacaciones en agosto.**
	mees ee-hos estan day bakathyones en agostoh
My birthday is in June.	**Mi cumpleaños es en junio.**
	mee koomplay-anyos es en hoonee-oh

LA HORA Y LOS NÚMEROS
Time and numbers

The hour is preceded by **la** as in **la una** (*one o'clock*) and **las** for the other numbers: **las dos**, **las tres**, and so on. In English the minutes come first: ten to five, in Spanish the hour comes first: **las cinco menos diez** (*five minus ten*).

2 **Words to remember: time** (4 minutes)

Memorize how to tell the time in Spanish.

la una *lah oonah*	one o'clock
la una y cinco *lah oonah ee theenkoh*	five past one
la una y cuarto *lah oonah ee kwartoh*	quarter past one
la una y veinte *lah oonah ee beyntay*	twenty past one
la una y media *lah oonah ee medee-ah*	half past one
las dos menos cuarto *las dos menos kwartoh*	quarter to two
las dos menos diez *las dos menos dyeth*	ten to two

3 **Useful phrases** (2 minutes)

Learn these phrases and then test yourself using the cover flap.

¿Qué hora es? *kay orah es*	What time is it?
¿A qué hora quiere el desayuno? *ah kay orah kyairay el desah-yoonoh*	What time do you want breakfast?
La reunión es a mediodía. *lah reh-oonyon es ah maydyodee-ah*	The meeting is at midday.

4 Words to remember: higher numbers (6 minutes)

To say 21 you use **veinti** and add **uno** (one): **veintiuno**. Successive numbers are created in the same way – for example, **veintidós** (22), **veintitrés** (23), and so on. After 30 link the numbers with **y** (and): **treinta y uno** (31), **cuarenta y cinco** (45), **sesenta y seis** (66).

Note the special forms used for 500, 700, and 900: **quinientos**, **setecientos**, and **novecientos**.

eleven	**once**	_onthay_
twelve	**doce**	_dothay_
thirteen	**trece**	_trethay_
fourteen	**catorce**	_katorthay_
fifteen	**quince**	_keenthay_
sixteen	**dieciséis**	_deeaytheeseyees_
seventeen	**diecisiete**	_deeaytheesyeytay_
eighteen	**dieciocho**	_deeaythyochoh_
nineteen	**diecinueve**	_deeaythynwebay_
twenty	**veinte**	_beyntay_
thirty	**treinta**	_treyntah_
forty	**cuarenta**	_kwarentah_
fifty	**cincuenta**	_theenkwentah_
sixty	**sesenta**	_sesentah_
seventy	**setenta**	_setentah_
eighty	**ochenta**	_ochentah_
ninety	**noventa**	_nobentah_
hundred	**cien**	_theeayn_
two hundred	**doscientos**	_dos-theeayntos_
five hundred	**quinientos**	_keeneeayntos_
thousand	**mil**	_meel_
two thousand	**dos mil**	_dos meel_
one million	**un millón**	_oon mee-yon_

Quiero el autobús cincuenta y tres.
kyairoh el aootoboos theenkwentah ee tres
I want the number 53 bus.

5 Say it (2 minutes)

25
68
84
91
five to ten
half past eleven
What time is lunch?

LAS CITAS
Appointments

Say the days of the week.
(pp.28-9)

Say "three o'clock".
(pp.30-1)

What's the Spanish for
"today", "tomorrow", and
"yesterday"? (pp.28-9)

Business in Spain is generally conducted more
formally than in Britain or the United States. The
Spanish also tend to leave the office for the lunch
hour, often having a sit-down meal. Remember to
use the formal forms of *you* (**usted**, **ustedes**) in
business situations.

Bienvenido.
byenveneedoh
Welcome.

2 **Useful phrases** (5 minutes)

Learn these phrases and then test yourself.

¿Nos reunimos mañana? *nos reh-ooneemos* *manyanah*	Shall we meet tomorrow?
¿Con quién? *kon kee-en*	With whom?
¿Cuándo está libre? *kwandoh esta leebray*	When are you free?
Lo siento, estoy **ocupado(-a).** *loh syentoh, estoy* *okoopadoh(-ah)*	I'm sorry, I am busy.
¿Qué tal el jueves? *keh tal el hwebes*	How about Thursday?
A mí me va bien. *ah mee may bah byen*	That's good for me.

**el apretón
de manos**
*el apreton
day manos*
handshake

3 **In conversation** (4 minutes)

**Buenos días. Tengo
una cita.**
*bwenos deeyas. tengoh
oonah theetah*

Good morning. I have
an appointment.

¿Con quién es la cita?
kon kee-en es lah theetah

With whom is
the appointment?

Con el Señor Montoya.
kon el senyor montoyah

With Mr Montoya.

4 Put into practice (5 minutes)

Join in this conversation. Read the Spanish beside the pictures on the left and then follow the instructions to make your reply. Then test yourself by concealing the answers on the right with the cover flap.

¿Nos reunimos el jueves?
nos reh-oo<u>nee</u>mos el <u>hwe</u>bes?

Shall we meet Thursday?

Say: Sorry, I'm busy.

Lo siento, estoy ocupado(-a).
loh <u>syen</u>toh, es<u>toy</u> okoo<u>pa</u>doh(-ah)

¿Cuándo está libre?
<u>kwan</u>doh es<u>ta</u> <u>lee</u>bray

When are you free?

Say: Tuesday afternoon.

El martes por la tarde.
el <u>martes</u> por lah <u>tar</u>day

A mí me va bien.
ah mee may bah byen

That's good for me.

Ask: At what time?

¿A qué hora?
ah kay <u>o</u>rah

A las cuatro, si a usted le va bien.
ah las <u>kwa</u>troh, see ah oos<u>ted</u> le bah byen

At four o'clock, if that's good for you.

Say: Yes, it's good for me.

Sí, me va bien.
see, may bah byen

Muy bien. ¿A qué hora?
mwee byen. ah kay <u>o</u>rah?

Very good. What time?

A las tres, pero llego un poco tarde.
ah las tres, <u>pe</u>roh <u>ye</u>goh oon <u>po</u>koh <u>tar</u>day

At three o'clock, but I'm a little late.

No se preocupe. Tome asiento, por favor.
noh say pre-oh<u>koo</u>pay. <u>to</u>may as<u>yain</u>toh, por fa<u>bor</u>

Don't worry. Take a seat, please.

POR TELÉFONO
On the telephone

1 **Warm up** (1 minute)

Say "I'm sorry". (pp.32-3)

What is the Spanish for "I'd like an appointment". (pp.32-3)

How do you say "when?" in Spanish? (pp.32-3)

The emergency number for police, ambulance, or fire services is 112. For directory enquiries dial 11818. Telephone cards can be used with public or private phones by tapping in a code. Available from newsagents and tobacconists, they are a cheap way to call overseas.

2 **Match and repeat** (4 minutes)

Match the numbered items to the Spanish in the panel on the left, then test yourself.

1 el cargador
   el kargador

2 el contestador automático
   el kontestador aootomateekoh

3 la tarjeta telefónica
   lah tarhetah telefoneekah

4 el móvil
   el mobeel

5 los auriculares
   los aooreekoolares

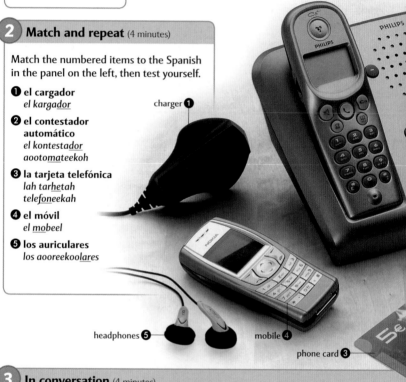

charger **1**

headphones **5**

mobile **4**

phone card **3**

3 **In conversation** (4 minutes)

Dígame, Susana Castillo al habla.
deegamay, soosanah kasteeyoh al ablah

Hello. Susana Castillo speaking.

Buenos días. Quisiera hablar con Julián López, por favor.
bwenos deeyas. keesyair-ah ablar kon hooleean lopeth, por fabor

Hello. I'd like to speak to Julián López, please.

¿De parte de quién?
day partay day kee-en?

Who's speaking?

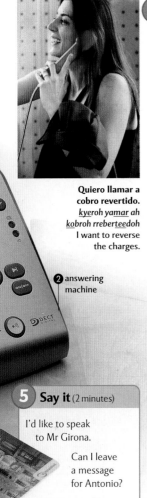

Quiero llamar a cobro revertido.
kyeroh yamar ah kobroh rreberteedoh
I want to reverse the charges.

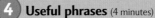
answering machine

4 Useful phrases (4 minutes)

Practise these phrases and then test yourself using the cover flap.

Quisiera una línea externa.
keesyairah oonah leeneah externah

I'd like an outside line.

Quisiera hablar con María Alfaro.
keesyairah ablar kon mareeah alfaroh

I'd like to speak to María Alfaro.

¿Puedo dejar un mensaje?
pwedoh dehar oon mensahay

Can I leave a message?

Perdone, me he equivocado de número.
perdonay, may ay ekeebokadoh day noomeroh

Sorry, I have the wrong number.

5 Say it (2 minutes)

I'd like to speak to Mr Girona.

Can I leave a message for Antonio?

José Ortega, de Imprentas Lacuesta.
hosay ortegah, day eemprentas lakwestah

José Ortega of Lacuesta Printers.

Lo siento. La línea está comunicando.
loh syaintoh. lah leeneah estah komooneekandoh

I'm sorry. The line is busy.

¿Le puede decir que me llame, por favor?
lay pweday detheer kay may yamay, por fabor

Can you ask him to call me, please?

REPASE Y REPITA
Review and repeat

1 Sums

❶ dieciséis
deeaytheesayees

❷ treinta y nueve
treyntah ee nwebay

❸ cincuenta y tres
theenkwentah ee tres

❹ setenta y cuatro
setentah ee kwatroh

❺ noventa y nueve
nobentah ee nwebay

1 Sums (4 minutes)

Say the answers to these sums out loud in Spanish. Then check you have remembered correctly.

❶ 10 + 6 = ?
❷ 14 + 25 = ?
❸ 66 – 13 = ?
❹ 40 + 34 = ?
❺ 90 + 9 = ?

3 Telephones (3 minutes)

What are the numbered items in Spanish?

❶ mobile

phone card ❸

2 I want…

❶ Quiere
kyairay

❷ quiere
kyairay

❸ queremos
keraymos

❹ quieres
kyaires

❺ quieren
kyairen

❻ quiero
kyairoh

2 I want… (3 minutes)

Fill the gaps with the correct form of (to want).

❶ ¿ _____ usted un café?
❷ Ella _____ ir de vacaciones.
❸ Nosotros _____ una mesa para tres.
❹ Tú _____ una cerveza.
❺ Ellos _____ una mesa para dos.
❻ Yo _____ caramelos.

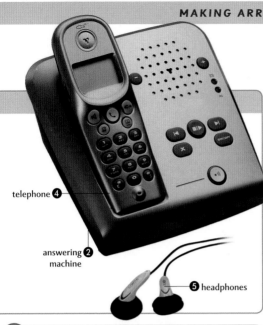

telephone ❹

answering ❷
machine

❺ headphones

3 Telephones

❶ **el móvil**
el mobeel

❷ **el contestador automático**
el kontestador aootomateekoh

❸ **la tarjeta telefónica**
lah tarhetah telefoneekah

❹ **el teléfono**
el telefonoh

❺ **los auriculares**
los aooreekoolares

---

4 When? (2 minutes)

What do these sentences mean?

❶ **Tengo una cita el lunes veinte de mayo.**

❷ **Mi cumpleaños es en septiembre.**

❸ **Hoy es domingo.**

❹ **No trabajo en agosto.**

4 When?

❶ I have a meeting on Monday, 20th May.
❷ My birthday is in September.
❸ Today is Sunday.
❹ I don't work in August.

---

5 Time (3 minutes)

Say these times in Spanish.

5 Time

❶ **la una**
lah oonah

❷ **la una y cinco**
la oonah ee theenkoh

❸ **la una y veinte**
lah oonah ee beyntay

❹ **la una y media**
lah oonah ee medee-ah

❺ **la una y cuarto**
lah oonah ee kwartoh

❻ **las dos menos diez**
las dos menos dyeth

EN LA OFICINA DE BILLETES
At the ticket office

Count to 100 in tens.
(pp.10-11, pp.30-1)

Ask "What time is it?"
(pp.30-1)

Say "Half-past one".
(pp.30-1)

In Spain, commuter trains are very good value, clean, and efficient. Long-distance trains still offer smoking and non-smoking carriages, and the prices vary depending on what day you travel, blue days being the cheapest.

2 **Words to remember** (3 minutes)

Learn these words and then test yourself.

el pasajero
el pasahairoh
passenger

la señal
lah senyal
sign

la estación lah estathyon	(train) station
la terminal lah termeenal	(bus) station
el billete el beeyetay	ticket
de ida day eedah	single
de ida y vuelta day eedah ee bweltah	return
de primera day preemerah	first class
de segunda day segoondah	second class
el descuento el deskwentoh	discount

La estación está llena de gente.
lah estathyon estah yenah day hentay
The station is crowded.

3 **In conversation** (4 minutes)

Dos billetes para Bilbao, por favor.
dos beeyetes parah beeba-oh, por fabor

Two tickets for Bilbao, please.

¿De ida y vuelta?
day eedah y bweltah

Return?

Si.¿Necesito reservar asiento?
see. netheseetoh rreseerbar asyaintoh

Yes. Do I need to reserve seats?

4 Useful phrases (5 minutes)

Learn these phrases and then test yourself using the cover flap.

Mi tren va con retraso.
mee tren bah kon rretrasoh
My train is late.

el tren	**el andén**
el tren	*el anden*
train	platform

How much is a ticket to Madrid?	**¿Cuánto cuesta un billete para Madrid?** *kwantoh kwaystah oon beeyetay parah madreed*
Can I pay by credit card?	**¿Puedo pagar con tarjeta de crédito?** *pwedoh pagar kon tarhetah day kredeetoh*
Do I have to change?	**¿Tengo que cambiar?** *tengoh kay kambee-ar*
Which platform does the train leave from?	**¿De qué andén sale el tren?** *day kay anden salay el tren*
Are there any discounts?	**¿Hay algún descuento?** *ah-ee algoon deskwentoh*
What time does the train for Gijón leave?	**¿A qué hora sale el tren para Gijón?** *ah kay orah salay el tren parah geehon*

5 Say it (2 minutes)

Which platform does the train for Madrid leave from?

Three return tickets to Murcia, please.

Cultural tip Most train stations now have automatic ticket machines that also take credit cards.

No hace falta. Cuarenta euros, por favor.
noh ahthay faltah. kwarentah eh-ooros, por fabor

That's not necessary. Forty euros, please.

¿Aceptan tarjetas de crédito?
ahtheptan tarhetas day kredeetoh

Do you accept credit cards?

Si. El tren sale del andén cinco.
see. el tren salay del anden theenkoh

Yes. The train leaves from platform five.

1 Warm up (1 minute)

What is "train" in Spanish? (pp.38-9)

What does "¿De qué andén sale el tren?" mean? (pp.38-9)

Ask "When are you free?" (pp.32-3)

IR Y COGER
To go and to take

The verbs **ir** (*to go*) and **coger** (*to take*) allow you to create many useful sentences. Note that **coger** can also mean to catch: **coger una pelota** (*to catch a ball*), **coger un resfriado** (*to catch a cold*); to grab: **coger a alguien** (*to grab someone*); and to hold: **coger a un bebé** (*to hold a baby*).

2 Ir: to go (6 minutes)

Spanish uses the same form of **ir** for both *I go* and *I am going*: **voy a Madrid** (*I am going to Madrid/I go to Madrid*). The same is true of other verbs - for example, **cojo el metro** (*I am taking the metro/I take the metro*).

yo voy *yoh boy*	I go
tú vas/usted va *too bas/oosted bah*	you go (informal/formal singular)
él/ella va *el/eh-yah bah*	he/she goes
nosotros(-as) vamos *nosotros(-as) bamos*	we go
vosotros(-as) vais/ustedes van *bosotros(-as) baees/oostedes ban*	you go (informal/formal plural)
ellos/ellas van *eh-yos/eh-yas ban*	they go

¿A dónde vas? *ah donday bas*	Where are you going?
Voy a Madrid. *boy ah madreed*	I am going to Madrid.

Voy a la Plaza de España.
boy ah lah plathah day espanyah
I am going to the Plaza de España.

Conversational tip You may have noticed that **de** (*of*) combines with **el** to produce **del** as in **Museo del Prado** (meaning literally *museum of the Prado*); **el menú del día** (*menu of the day*). In the same way, **a** (*to*) combines with **el** to produce **al**: **Voy al museo** (*I'm going to the museum*). With feminine and plural words **de** remains separate from **la**, **los**, and **las**.

3 Coger: to take (6 minutes)

Say the present tense of **coger** (*to take*) aloud. Use the cover flap to test yourself. When you are confident, practise the sentences below.

yo cojo *yoh kohoh*	I take
tú coges/usted coge *too kohes/oosted kohay*	you take (informal/ formal singular)
él/ella coge *el/eh-yah kohay*	he/she takes
nosotros(-as) cogemos *nosotros(-as) kohaymos*	we take
vosotros(-as) cogéis/ ustedes cogen *bosotros(-as) kohe-ees/ oostedes kohen*	you take (informal/ formal plural)
ellos/ellas cogen *eh-yos/eh-yas kohen*	they take

**Yo cojo el metro todos
los días.**
*yoh kohoh el metroh todos
los deeyas*
I take the metro every day.

No quiero coger un taxi. *noh kyairoh koher oon taksee*	I don't want to take a taxi.
Coja la primera a la izquierda. *kohah lah preemerah ah lah eethkyairdah*	Take the first on the left.

4 Put into practice (2 minutes)

Cover the text on the right and complete the dialogue in Spanish.

¿A dónde va? *ah donday bah*	**Voy a la Puerta del Sol.** *boy ah lah pwertah del sol*
Where are you going?	
Say: I'm going to the Puerta del Sol.	
¿Quiere coger el autobús? *kyairay koher el aootoboos*	**No, quiero ir en metro.** *noh, kyairoh eer en metroh*
Do you want to take the bus?	
Say: No, I want to go by metro.	

1 Warm up (1 minute)

Say "I don't want to take a taxi". (pp.40-41)

Ask "Where are you going?" (pp.40-41)

Say "80" and "40". (pp.30-31)

TAXI, AUTOBÚS, Y METRO
Taxi, bus, and metro

The metro and some buses operate a ticket system where you have to validate your tickets in a machine. There's a standard fare per ride, but you can also buy a **metrobús**, a book of 10 tickets for both buses and metro.

2 Words to remember (4 minutes)

Familiarize yourself with these words.

el autobús *el aootoboos*	bus/coach
la taquilla *lah takeeyah*	ticket office
la estación de metro *lah estathyon day metroh*	metro station
la parada de autobús *lah paradah day aootoboos*	bus stop
la tarifa *lah tareefah*	fare
el taxi *el taksee*	taxi
la parada de taxis *lah paradah day taksees*	taxi rank

¿Para aquí el 17?
parah ahkee el deeaytheeseeaytay
Does the number 17 bus stop here?

3 In conversation: taxi (2 minutes)

A la Plaza de España, por favor.
ah lah plathah day espanyah, por fabor

Plaza de España, please.

Sí, de acuerdo, señor.
see, day akwairdo, senyor

Yes, certainly, sir.

¿Me puede dejar aquí, por favor?
may pweday dehar ahkee, por fabor

Can you drop me here, please?

4 Useful phrases (4 minutes)

Practise these phrases and then test yourself using the cover flap.

I'd like a taxi to go to the Prado.	**Quisiera un taxi para ir al Prado.** keesyairah oon taksee parah eer al prado
When is the next bus?	**¿Cuándo sale el próximo autobús?** kwandoh salay el prokseemoh aootoboos
How do you get to the museum?	**¿Cómo se va al museo?** komoh say bah al moosayoh
How long is the journey?	**¿Cuánto dura el viaje?** kwantoh doorah el beeahay
Please wait for me.	**Espéreme, por favor.** esperemay, por fabor

Cultural tip Metro lines in Madrid are known by numbers and the names of the first and last stations. Look out for the relevant end station. The Madrid metro runs every day between 6.00am and 2.00am.

6 Say it (2 minutes)

Do you go near the train station?

Do you go near the Prado?

When is the next bus to Barcelona?

5 In conversation: bus (2 minutes)

¿Pasa cerca del museo?
pasah therkah del moosayoh

Do you go near the museum?

Sí. Son 80 céntimos.
see. son ochentah thenteemos

Yes. That's 80 cents.

Avíseme cuando lleguemos.
abeesemay kwandoh yeghemos

Tell me when we arrive.

1 Warm up (1 minute)

How do you say "I have..."? (pp.14-15)

Say "my father", "my sister", and "my parents". (pp.10-11, pp.12-13)

Say "I'm going to Madrid". (pp.40-1)

EN LA CARRETERA
On the road

Spanish **autopistas** (*motorways*) are fast but can be quite expensive. You will find signs for **el peaje** (*toll payment stations*). These have multiple lanes. Make sure you enter a green lane that allows payment by cash or credit card. Some lanes are for passholders or lorries only.

2 Match and repeat (4 minutes)

Match the numbered items to the list on the left, then test yourself.

❶ **el maletero**
el malaytairoh

❷ **el parabrisas**
el parabreesas

❸ **el capó**
el kapoh

❹ **la rueda**
lah rwedah

❺ **el neumático**
el ne-oomateekoh

❻ **la puerta**
lah pwertah

❼ **los faros**
los faros

❽ **el parachoques**
el parachokes

❶ boot

wheel ❹

tyre ❺

door ❻

Cultural tip Some self-service petrol stations can be unmanned. In this case, you usually have to specify how many litres you want and pay by card before filling up.

3 Road features (2 minutes)

la rotonda
lah rrotonduh

roundabout

el semáforo
el semaforoh

traffic lights

el cruce
el kroothay

intersection

4 Useful phrases (4 minutes)

Learn these phrases and then test yourself using the cover flap.

The indicator doesn't work.	**El intermitente no funciona.** *el intairmeetaintay noh foonthyonah*
Fill it up, please.	**Lleno, por favor.** *yennoh, por fabor*

2 windscreen

3 bonnet

headlights **7**   **8** bumper

5 Match and repeat (3 minutes)

Familiarize yourself with these words then test yourself using the flap.

petrol	**la gasolina** *lah gasoleenah*
diesel	**el gasoil** *el gasoil*
oil	**el aceite** *el ah-thayeetay*
engine	**el motor** *el motor*
gearbox	**la caja de cambios** *lah kahah day kambyos*
indicator	**el intermitente** *el intairmeetaintay*
flat tyre	**la rueda pinchada** *lah rwaydah peenchadah*
exhaust	**el tubo de escape** *el tooboh day eskapay*
driving licence	**el carné de conducir** *el karnay day kondootheer*

6 Say it (1 minute)

There's something wrong with my engine.

I have a flat tyre.

la autopista
lah aootopeestah

motorway/expressway

la autopista de peaje
lah aootopeestah day pyahay

toll motorway

el atasco de tráfico
el ataskoh day trafeekoh

traffic jam

REPASE Y REPITA
Review and repeat

Respuestas
Answers (Cover with flap)

1 Transport

❶ el autobús
el aootoboos

❷ el taxi
el taksee

❸ el coche
el kochay

❹ la bicicleta
lah beetheekletah

❺ el metro
el metroh

1 Transport (3 minutes)

Name these forms of transport in Spanish.

bus ❶

metro ❺

2 Go and take

❶ ir
eer

❷ cojo
kohoh

❸ va
bah

❹ vamos
bamos

❺ cogen
kohen

❻ voy
boy

2 Go and take (4 minutes)

Use the correct form of the verb in brackets.

❶ Quiero ____ a la estación. (ir)

❷ Yo ____ el metro. (coger)

❸ ¿A dónde ____ usted? (ir)

❸ Nosotros ____ al Museo del Prado. (ir)

❺ Ellos ____ un taxi. (coger)

❻ Yo ____ a Madrid. (ir)

2 taxi

3 car

4 bicycle

3 You (4 minutes)

Use the correct form for **usted** or **tú** in each sentence.

❶ You are in a café. Ask "Do you have churros?"

❷ You are with a friend. Ask "Do you want a beer?"

❸ A visitor approaches you at your company reception. Ask "Do you have an appointment?"

❹ You are on the bus. Ask "Do you go near the station?"

❺ Ask your friend where she's going tomorrow.

Respuestas
Answers (Cover with flap)

3 You

❶ ¿Tiene churros?
tyenay choorros

❷ ¿Quieres una cerveza?
kyaires oonah thairbaythah

❸ ¿Tiene una cita?
tyenay oonah theetah

❹ ¿Pasa cerca de la estación?
pasah therkah day lah estathyon

❺ ¿A dónde vas mañana?
ah donday bas manyanah

4 Tickets (4 minutes)

You're buying tickets at a train station. Follow the conversation, replying in Spanish following the numbered English prompts.

¿Qué desea?
❶ I'd like two tickets to Sevilla.

¿De ida o de ida y vuelta?
❷ Return, please.

Muy bien. Cincuenta euros, por favor.
❸ What time does the train leave?

A las tres y diez.
❹ What platform does the train leave from?

Andén número siete.
❺ Thank you very much. Goodbye.

4 Tickets

❶ Quisiera dos billetes para Sevilla.
keesyairah dos beeyetes parah sebeeyah

❷ De ida y vuelta, por favor.
day eedah ee bweltah, por fabor

❸ ¿A qué hora sale el tren?
ah kay orah salay el tren

❹ ¿De qué andén sale el tren?
day kay anden salay el tren

❺ Muchas gracias. Adiós.
moochas grathyas. addy-os

1 Warm up (1 minute)

Ask "How do you get to the museum?" (pp.42-3)

Say "I want to take the metro" and "I don't want to take a taxi". (pp.40-1)

EN LA CIUDAD
About town

Note that the Spanish word **museo** (*museum*) also means art gallery when it's a public building in which works of art are exhibited; **galería de arte** usually refers to a shop that sells works of art. Be careful, too, not to confuse **librería** (*bookshop* or *bookshelf*) and **biblioteca** (*library*).

2 Match and repeat (4 minutes)

Match the numbered locations to the words in the panel.

1 **el ayuntamiento**
el ahyoonta-myaintoh

2 **el puente**
el pwentay

3 **el centro**
el thentroh

4 **la iglesia**
lah eegleseeah

5 **la plaza**
lah plathah

6 **el aparcamiento**
el aparka-myaintoh

7 **la biblioteca**
lah bibleeotekah

8 **el museo**
el moosayoh

1 town hall   church **4**

city centre **3**

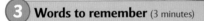

3 Words to remember (3 minutes)

Familiarize yourself with these words and test yourself using the cover flap.

la gasolinera *lah gasoleenerah*	petrol station
la oficina de información turística *lah ohfeetheenah day eenformathyon tooreesteekah*	tourist information
la piscina municipal *lah pistheenah mooneetheepal*	public swimming pool

5 square

7 library

Conversational tip In Spanish there are two ways of saying *am*, *is*, or *are*. You have already learned the verb **ser** (p.14): **soy inglés** (*I am English*); **es vegetariano** (*he is vegetarian*). When talking about where something is, you need to use a different verb: **estar**. The most important forms of this verb are: **estoy** (*I am*), **está** (*he/she/it is*), and **están** (*they are*): **¿Dónde están lla iglesia?** (*Where is the church?*); **El café no está lejos.** (*The café isn't far.*)

4 Useful phrases (4 minutes)

La catedral está en el centro.
lah katedral estah en el thentroh
The cathedral is in the
city centre.

Practise these phrases and then test yourself using the cover flap.

Is there an art gallery in town?	**¿Hay algún museo de arte en la ciudad?** *ah-ee algoon moosayoh day artay en lah thyoodad*
Is it far from here?	**¿Está lejos de aquí?** *estah lehos day ahkee*
There is a swimming pool near the bridge.	**Hay una piscina cerca del puente.** *ah-ee oonah peestheenah therkah del pwentay*

5 Put into practice (3 minutes)

bridge ②

car park ⑥

museum ⑧

Join in this conversation. Read the Spanish on the left and follow the instructions to make your reply. Then test yourself.

¿Le puedo ayudar? *lay pwedoh ahyoodar* Can I help you? Ask: Is there a library in town?	**¿Hay alguna biblioteca en la ciudad?** *ah-ee algoonah beebleeotekah en lah thyoodad*
No, pero hay un museo. *noh, peroh ah-ee oon moosayoh* No, but there's a museum. Ask: How do I get to the museum?	**¿Cómo se va al museo?** *komoh say bah al moosayoh*
Está por allí. *estah por ahyee* It's over there. Say: Thank you very much.	**Muchas gracias.** *moochas grathyas*

LAS DIRECCIONES
Directions

1 **Warm up** (1 minute)

How do you say "near the station"? (pp.42-3)

Say "Take the first on the left". (pp.40-1)

Ask "Where are you going?" (pp.40-1)

You'll often be able to find a **plano de la ciudad** (*town map*) in the town centre, usually near the town hall or tourist office. In the older parts of Spanish towns there are often narrow streets, where you will usually find a one-way system in operation. Parking is usually restricted.

2 **Useful phrases** (4 minutes)

Learn these phrases and then test yourself.

Tuerza a la izquierda/ derecha. *twerthah ah lah eethkyairdah/derechah*	Turn left/right.
todo recto *todoh rrektoh*	straight on
¿Cómo se va a la piscina? *komoh say bah ah lah peestheenah*	How do I get to the swimming pool?
la primera a la derecha *lah preemerah ah lah derechah*	first right
la segunda a la izquierda *lah segoondah ah lah eethkyairdah*	second left

el bloque de oficinas
el blokay day ohfeetheenas
office block

la fuente
lah fwentay
fountain

3 **In conversation** (4 minutes)

¿Hay un restaurante en la ciudad?
ah-ee oon restaoorantay en la thyoodad

Is there a restaurant nearby?

Sí, cerca de la estación.
see, therkah day lah estathyon

Yes, near the station.

¿Cómo se va a la estación?
komoh say bah ah lah estathyon

How do I get to the station?

4 Words to remember (4 minutes)

Me he perdido.
may eh perdeedoh
I'm lost.

el centro deportivo
el thentroh deporteeboh
leisure centre

Familiarize yourself with these words and test
yourself using the flap.

traffic lights	**el semáforo** *el semaforoh*
corner	**la esquina** *lah eskeenah*
street/road	**la calle** *lah kayay*
main road	**la calle principal** *lah kayay preentheepal*
at the end of the street	**al final de la calle** *al feenal day lah kayay*
map	**el plano** *el planoh*
flyover	**el paso elevado** *el pasoh elebadoh*
opposite	**enfrente de** *enfrentay day*

la zona peatonal
lah thonah pe-ahtonal
pedestrian zone

¿Dondé estamos?
donday estamos
Where are we?

5 Say it (2 minutes)

Turn right at the end
of the street.

Turn left opposite
the museum.

It's ten minutes by bus.

**Tuerza a la izquierda en
el semáforo.**
*twerthah ah lah
eethkyairdah en el semaforoh*

Turn left at the traffic lights.

¿Está lejos?
estah lehos

Is it far?

**No, cinco minutos
andando.**
*noh, theenkoh meenootos
andandoh*

No, it's five minutes
on foot.

EL TURISMO
Sightseeing

Most national museums and art galleries close on Mondays and public holidays. Although shops are normally closed on Sundays, many will open in tourist areas. In provincial areas, it is not unusual for public buildings and shops to close at lunchtime, between 1.30 and 4.30pm.

1 Warm up (1 minute)

Say the days of the week in Spanish. (pp.28-9)

How do you say "six o'clock"? (pp.30-1)

Ask "What time is it?" (pp.30-1)

2 Words to remember (4 minutes)

Familiarize yourself with these words and test yourself using the flap.

la guía *lah gheeah*	guidebook
la entrada *lah entradah*	entrance ticket
el horario de apertura *el oraryoh day apertoorah*	opening times
el día festivo *el deeyah festeevoh*	public holiday
entrada libre *entradah leebray*	free entrance

la visita con guía
lah beeseetah kon gheeah
guided tour

Cultural tip If a public holiday falls on a Thursday or a Tuesday, people will often **hacer puente** (do a bridge) - in other words, they take Friday or Monday off as well, to make a long weekend.

3 In conversation (3 minutes)

¿Abren esta tarde?
ahbren estah tarday

Do you open this afternoon?

Sí, pero cerramos a las cuatro.
see, peroh therramos ah las kwatroh

Yes, but we close at four o'clock.

¿Tienen acceso para sillas de ruedas?
tyenen akthesoh parah seeyas day rwedas

Do you have access for wheelchairs?

4 Useful phrases (3 minutes)

Practise these phrases and then test yourself using the cover flap.

What time do you open/close?	**¿A qué hora abre/cierra?** *ah kay orah ahbray/ thyairrah*
Where are the toilets?	**¿Dónde están los servicios?** *donday estan los serbeethyos*
Is there access for wheelchairs?	**¿Hay acceso para sillas de ruedas?** *ah-ee akthesoh parah seeyas day rwedas*

5 Put into practice (4 minutes)

Cover the text on the right and complete the dialogue in Spanish.

Lo siento, el museo está cerrado. *loh syentoh, el moosayoh estah therradoh*

Sorry. The museum is closed.

Ask: Do you open on Tuesdays?

¿Abren los martes? *ahbren los martes*

Sí, pero cerramos temprano. *see, peroh therramos tempranoh*

Yes, but we close early.

Ask: At what time?

¿A qué hora? *ah kay orah*

Sí, el ascensor está allí. *see, el asthensor estah ah-yee*

Yes, there's a lift over there.

Gracias, quisiera cuatro entradas. *grathyas, keesyairah kwatroh entradas*

Thank you, I'd like four entrance tickets.

Aquí tiene, y la guía es gratis. *ahkee tyenay, ee lah gheeah es gratees*

Here you are, and the guidebook is free.

EN EL AEROPUERTO
At the airport

Say "half past one".
(pp.30-1)

What's the Spanish for
"ticket"? (pp.38-9)

Say "I am going to New
York". (pp.40-1)

Although the airport environment is largely
international, it is sometimes useful to be able to
ask your way around the terminal in Spanish. It's a
good idea to make sure you have a few coins when
you arrive at the airport; you may need to pay for
a luggage trolley.

2 **Words to remember** (4 minutes)

Familiarize yourself with these words and
test yourself using the flap.

la facturación *lah faktoorathyon*	check-in
las salidas *las saleedas*	departures
las llegadas *las yehgadas*	arrivals
la aduana *lah adwanah*	customs
el control de pasaportes *el kontrol day pasaportes*	passport control
la terminal *lah termeenal*	terminal
la puerta de embarque *lah pwertah day embarkay*	boarding gate

**¿Cuál es la puerta de embarque
para el vuelo veintitrés?**
*kwal es lah pwertah day embarkay
parah el bweloh bayeenteetres*
Which is the boarding gate
for flight 23?

3 **Useful phrases** (3 minutes)

Learn these phrases and then test yourself
using the cover flap.

¿Sale a su hora el vuelo para Sevilla? *salay ah soo orah el bweloh parah seveeyah*	Is the flight for Seville on time?
No encuentro mi equipaje. *noh enkwentroh mee ehkeepahay*	I can't find my luggage.

4 Put into practice (3 minutes)

Join in this conversation. Read the Spanish on the left and follow the instructions to make your reply. Then test yourself by concealing the answers using the cover flap.

Hola, ¿le puedo ayudar?
o-lah, lay pwedoh ahyoodar

Hello, can I help you?

Ask: Is the flight to Madrid on time?

¿Sale a su hora el vuelo para Madrid?
salay ah soo orah el bweloh parah madreed

Sí señor.
see senyor

Yes sir.

Ask: Which is the boarding gate?

¿Cuál es la puerta de embarque?
kwal es lah pwertah day embarkay

5 Match and repeat (4 minutes)

Match the numbered items to the Spanish words in the panel.

❶ la tarjeta de embarque
lah tarhetah day embarkay

❷ el mostrador de facturación
el mostrador day faktoorathyon

❸ el billete
el beeyehtay

❹ el pasaporte
el pasaportay

❺ la maleta
lah malaytah

❻ el equipaje de mano
el ehkeepahay day manoh

❼ el carrito
el karreetoh

boarding ❶ pass

check-in ❷ desk

ticket ❸

passport ❹

❼ trolley

❺ suitcase   ❻ hand luggage

REPASE Y REPITA
Review and repeat

Respuestas
Answers (Cover with flap)

1 Places

❶ el museo
el moosayoh

❷ el ayuntamiento
el ahyoonta-myaintoh

❸ el puente
el pwentay

❹ la biblioteca
lah beeblee-ohtekah

❺ el aparcamiento
el ahparka-myaintoh

❻ la catedral
lah katedral

❼ la plaza
lah plathah

1 Places (4 minutes)

Name the numbered places in Spanish.

 ❶ museum

 ❷ town hall

 ❸ bridge

 ❹ library

 ❺ car park

 ❻ cathedral

square ❼

2 Car parts

❶ el parabrisas
el parabreesas

❷ el intermitente
el intairmee-taintay

❸ el capó
el kapoh

❹ el neumático
el ne-oomateekoh

❺ la puerta
lah pwertah

❻ el parachoques
el parachokes

2 Car parts (3 minutes)

Name these car parts in Spanish.

windscreen ❶

❹ tyre   ❺ door

Respuestas
Answers (Cover with flap)

3 Questions (4 minutes)

Ask the questions that match these answers.

❶ **El autobús sale a las ocho.**
el aootoboos salay ah las ochoh

❷ **El café es un euro cincuenta.**
el kafay es oon eh-ooro theenkwentah

❸ **No, no quiero vino.**
noh, noh kyairoh beenoh

❹ **El tren sale del andén cinco.**
el tren salay del anden theenkoh

❺ **Nosotros vamos a León.**
nosotros bamos ah leh-on

❻ **El próximo tren es dentro
de quince minutos.**
*el prokseemoh tren es dentroh
day keenthay meenootos*

3 Questions

❶ **¿A qué hora sale
el autobús?**
*ah kay orah salay
el aootoboos*

❷ **¿Cuánto es el café?**
kwantoh es el kafay

❸ **¿Quieres vino?**
kyaires beenoh

❹ **¿De qué andén sale
el tren?**
*day kay anden salay
el tren*

❺ **¿A dónde vais?**
ah donday baees

❻ **¿Cuándo es el
próximo tren?**
*kwandoh es el
prokseemoh tren*

❷ indicator

❸ bonnet

❻ bumper

4 Verbs (4 minutes)

Choose the correct
form of the verb in
brackets to fill the gaps.

❶ **Yo _____ inglés. (ser)**

❷ **Nosotros _____ el
metro. (tomar)**

❸ **Ella _____ a Marbella.
(ir)**

❹ **Él _____ casado.
(estar)**

❺ **¿Tú _____ un té?
(querer)**

❻ **¿Cuántos niños _____
usted? (tener)**

4 Verbs

❶ **soy**
soy

❷ **cogemos**
kohaymos

❸ **va**
bah

❹ **está**
estah

❺ **quieres**
kyaires

❻ **tiene**
tyenay

<table>
<tr><td>

1 Warm up (1 minute)

Ask "Do you accept credit cards?" (pp.38-9)

Ask "How much is that?" (pp.18-19)

Ask "Do you have children?" (pp.10-11)

</td><td>

RESERVAR UNA HABITACIÓN
Booking a room

Types of accommodation in Spain include: **hotel**, categorized from one to five stars; **pensión**, a small family-run hotel; **hostal**, cheap and basic; and **parador**, state-owned hotels in historic properties or places of great beauty.

</td></tr>
</table>

2 Useful phrases (3 minutes)

Practise these phrases and then test yourself by concealing the Spanish on the left using the cover flap.

¿El desayuno está incluido?
el desayoonoh estah inklooeedoh

Is breakfast included?

¿Aceptan animales de compañía?
atheptan aneemales day kompanyeeah

Do you accept pets?

¿Tienen servicio de habitaciones?
tyenen serbeethyoh day abeetathyones

Do you have room service?

¿A qué hora tengo que dejar la habitación?
ah kay orah tengoh kay dehar lah abeetathyon

What time do I have to leave the room?

3 In conversation (5 minutes)

¿Tiene habitaciones libres?
tyenay abeetathyones leebres

Do you have any vacancies?

Sí, una habitación doble.
see, oonah abeetathyon doblay

Yes, a double room.

¿Tiene una cuna?
tyenay oonah koonah

Do you have a cot?

4 Words to remember (4 minutes)

Familiarize yourself with these words and test yourself by concealing the Spanish on the right using the cover flap.

room	**la habitación** *lah abeetathyon*
single room	**la habitación individual** *lah abeetathyon indeebeedwal*
double room	**la habitación doble** *lah abeetathyon doblay*
bathroom	**el cuarto de baño** *el kwartoh day banyoh*
shower	**la ducha** *lah doochah*
breakfast	**el desayuno** *el desayoonoh*
key	**la llave** *lah yabay*
balcony	**el balcón** *el balkon*
air-conditioning	**el aire acondicionado** *el ah-eeray akondeethyonadoh*

¿Tiene la habitación vistas al parque?
tyenay lah abeetathyon beestas al parkay
Does the room have a view over the park?

5 Say it (2 minutes)

Do you have a single room, please?

For six nights.

Is breakfast included?

Cultural tip Large hotels and **paradors** are generally the only types of hotel to offer breakfast, but you will generally be charged extra for it. If your accommodation doesn't provide breakfast, you'll usually find it easy to discover a bar or a café nearby where you can go for **café con leche** in the mornings.

Sí, claro. ¿Cuántas noches?
see, klaroh. kwantas noches

Yes, of course. How many nights?

Para tres noches.
parah tres noches

For three nights.

Muy bien. Aquí tiene la llave.
mwee byen. ahkee tyenay lah yabay

Very good. Here's the key.

EN EL HOTEL
In the hotel

1 Warm up (1 minute)

Say "Is there...?" and
"There isn't...". (pp.48-9)

What does "¿Le puedo
ayudar?" mean? (pp.54-5)

Although the larger hotels almost always
have en-suite bathrooms, there are still some
pensiones and **hostales** where you will have
to share bathroom facilities and which usually
don't provide towels. It is always advisable to
check what is provided when you book.

2 Match and repeat (6 minutes)

Match the numbered items in this hotel bedroom with the
Spanish text in the panel and test yourself using the cover flap.

❶ **la mesilla de noche**
*lah meseeyah day
nochay*

❷ **la lámpara**
lah lamparah

❸ **el equipo de música**
*el ekeepoh day
mooseekah*

❹ **las cortinas**
las korteenas

❺ **el sofá**
el sofah

❻ **la almohada**
lah almoh-ahdah

❼ **el cojín**
el koheen

❽ **la cama**
lah kamah

❾ **la colcha**
lah kolchah

❿ **la manta**
lah mantah

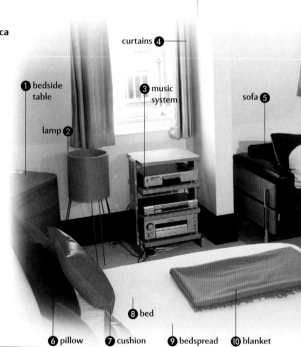

curtains ❹

❶ bedside table

❸ music system

sofa ❺

lamp ❷

❻ pillow   ❼ cushion   ❾ bedspread   ❿ blanket

❽ bed

Cultural tip When you arrive in your double room, you will
usually see one long pillow instead of two individual ones on
the bed. This is the usual pillow for a double bed - **cama de
matrimonio** (literally, *marriage bed*). If you don't want to share your
bed or pillow, you'll have to ask for **una habitación doble con
dos camas** (*a double room with two beds*) to get a twin room.

3 Useful phrases (5 minutes)

Practise these phrases and then test yourself using the cover flap.

The room is too cold/hot. **Hace demasiado frío/ calor en la habitación.**
ahthay daymasyahdoh freeoh/kalor en lah abeetathyon

There are no towels. **No hay toallas.**
noh ah-ee toh-ahyas

I need some soap. **Necesito jabón.**
netheseetoh habon

The shower doesn't work. **La ducha no funciona.**
lah doochah noh foonthyonah

The lift is broken. **El ascensor está roto.**
el asthensor estah rrotoh

4 Put into practice (3 minutes)

Practise these phrases and then complete the dialogue in Spanish.

¿Le atienden? **Necesito almohadas.**
lay atyainden *netheseetoh almoh-ahdas*

Can I help you?

Say: I need some pillows.

La camarera se las llevará. **Y la televisión no**
lah kamarairah say **funciona.**
las yebarah *ee lah telebeesyon noh foonthyonah*

The maid will bring some.

Say: And the TV doesn't work.

EN EL CÁMPING
At the campsite

1 **Warm up** (1 minute)

How do you ask
"Can I?" (pp.34-5)

Say "The lift is broken".
(pp.60-1)

Say "I need some towels".
(pp.60-1)

Camping is very popular in Spain. The country's
numerous campsites are well organized and operate
on a star system. The local tourist information office
will be able to offer a list of campsites in the area
together with their ratings. It is advisable to book
in advance during the summer months.

2 **Useful phrases** (3 minutes)

Learn these phrases and then test
yourself by concealing the Spanish
with the cover flap.

¿Puedo alquilar una bicicleta? _pwedoh alkeelar oonah beetheekletah_	Can I rent a bicycle?
¿Es el agua potable? _es el ahgwah potablay_	Is this drinking water?
¿Se permiten hogueras? _say permeeten ohgheras_	Are campfires allowed?
Las radios están prohibidas. _las rradyos estan proheebeedas_	Radios are forbidden.

¿Dónde está el grifo?
donday estah el greefoh
Where is the tap?

la oficina
lah ofeetheenah
office

el contenedor de la basura
el kontenedor day lah basoorah
litter bin

el doble techo
el doblay taychoh
fly sheet

3 **In conversation** (5 minutes)

Necesito una plaza para tres noches.
netheseetoh oonah plathah parah tres noches

I need a pitch for
three nights.

Hay una cerca de la piscina.
ah-ee oonah therkah day lah peestheenah

There's one near the
swimming pool.

¿Cuánto cuesta para una roulotte?
kwantoh kwestah parah oonah rroolot

How much is it for
a caravan?

5 Say it (2 minutes)

I need a pitch for four nights.

Can I rent a tent?

Where's the electrical hook-up?

los aseos
los asayos
toilets

el punto de luz
el poontoh
day looth
electrical hook-up

la cuerda
lah kwerdah
guy rope

la clavija
la klabeehah
tent peg

4 Words to remember (4 minutes)

Learn these words and then test yourself using the cover flap.

campsite	**el cámping** *el kampeen*
tent	**la tienda** *lah tyendah*
caravan	**la roulotte** *lah rroolot*
camper van	**la autocaravana** *la ah-ootokarabanah*
pitch	**la plaza** *lah plathah*
campfire	**la hoguera** *lah ohgherah*
drinking water	**el agua potable** *el ahgwah potablay*
rubbish	**la basura** *lah basoorah*
camping gas	**el camping-gas** *el kampeen gas*
showers	**las duchas** *las doochas*
sleeping bag	**el saco de dormir** *el sakoh day dormeer*
air mattress	**la colchoneta** *lah kolchonetah*
ground sheet	**el suelo aislante** *el sweloh ah-eeslantay*

Cincuenta euros. Una noche por adelantado.
theenkwentah eh-ooros. oonah nochay por adelantadoh

Fifty euros. One night in advance.

¿Puedo alquilar una barbacoa?
pwedoh alkeelar oonah barbakoh-ah

Can I rent a barbecue?

Sí, pero tiene que dejar una señal.
see, peroh tyenay kay dehar oonah senyal

Yes, but you must pay a deposit.

DESCRIPCIONES
Descriptions

1 Warm up (1 minute)

How do you say "hot" and "cold"? (pp.60-1)

What is the Spanish for "room", "bed", and "pillow"? (pp.60-1)

Adjectives are words used to describe things. In Spanish you generally put the adjective after the thing it describes in the same gender and number: **una bebida fría** (*a cold drink*, feminine singular); **un café frío** (*a cold coffee*, masculine singular); **dos bebidas frías** (*two cold drinks*, feminine plural).

2 Words to remember (7 minutes)

Adjectives change depending on whether the thing described is masculine (**el**) or feminine (**la**). Generally, a final **o** changes to **a** in the feminine, but if the adjective ends with **e** (such as **grande**) it doesn't change for the feminine. To form the plural, just add an **s**.

duro/dura *dooroh/doorah*	hard
blando/blanda *blandoh/blandah*	soft
caliente *kalyaintay*	hot
frío/fría *freeoh/freeah*	cold
grande *granday*	big
pequeño/pequeña *pekenyoh/pekenyah*	small
bonito/bonita *boneetoh/boneetah*	beautiful
feo/fea *feh-oh/feh-ah*	ugly
ruidoso/ruidosa *rrweedosoh/rrweedosah*	noisy
tranquilo/tranquila *trankeeloh/trankeelah*	quiet
bueno/buena *bwenoh/bwenah*	good
malo/mala *maloh/malah*	bad
lento/lenta *lentoh/lentah*	slow
rápido/rápida *rrapeedoh/rrapeedah*	fast

las montañas altas
las montanyas altas
high mountains

la tienda pequeña
lah tyaindah pekenyah
small shop

el coche viejo
el koche bee-ayhoh
old car

El pueblo es muy bonito.
el pwebloh es mwee boneetoh
The village is very beautiful.

la calle tranquila
lah kayay trankeelah
quiet road

3 Useful phrases (4 minutes)

Learn these phrases. Note that you can emphasize a description by using **muy** (*very*), **demasiado** (*too*), or **más** (*more*) before the adjective.

This coffee is cold.	**Este café está frío.** *estay kafay estah free-oh*
My room is very noisy.	**Mi habitación es muy ruidosa.** *mee abeetathyon es mwee rrweedosah*
My car is too small.	**Mi coche es demasiado pequeño.** *mee koche es demasyahdoh pekenyoh*
I need a softer bed.	**Necesito una cama más blanda.** *netheseetoh oonah kamah mas blandah*

4 Put into practice (3 minutes)

Join in this conversation. Cover up the text on the right and complete the dialogue in Spanish. Check and repeat if necessary.

Ésta es la habitación.
estah es lah abeetathyon
This is the bedroom.
Say: The view is very beautiful.

La vista es muy bonita.
lah beestah es mwee boneetah

El cuarto de baño está por ahí.
el kwartoh day banyoh estah por ah-ee
The bathroom is over there.
Say: It is too small.

Es demasiado pequeño.
es demasyahdoh pekenyoh

No tenemos otra.
noh tenaymos otrah
We haven't another.
Say: It doesn't matter. We'll take the room.

No importa. Nos quedamos con la habitación.
noh importah. nos kedamos kon lah abeetathyon

Respuestas
Answers (Cover with flap)

REPASE Y REPITA
Review and repeat

1 Descriptions

❶ **caliente**
kalyaintay

❷ **pequeña**
pekenyah

❸ **frío**
free-oh

❹ **grande**
granday

❺ **tranquila**
trankeelah

1 Descriptions (3 minutes)

Put the word in brackets into Spanish. Use the correct masculine or feminine form.

❶ El agua está demasiado _____. (hot)

❷ La cama es muy _____. (small)

❸ El café está _____. (cold)

❹ Este cuarto de baño es más _____. (big)

❺ Quisiera una habitación más _____. (quiet)

2 Campsite

❶ **el punto de luz**
el poontoh day looth

❷ **la tienda**
lah tyaindah

❸ **el contenedor de la basura**
el kontenedor day lah basoorah

❹ **la cuerda**
lah kwerdah

❺ **los aseos**
los asayos

❻ **la roulotte**
lah rroolot

2 Campsite (3 minutes)

Name these items you might find in a campsite.

electrical ❶ hook-up

tent ❷

litter bin ❸

guy rope ❹

3 At the hotel (4 minutes)

You are booking a room in a hotel. Follow the conversation, replying in Spanish where you can see the English prompts.

¿Qué desean?
❶ Do you have any vacancies?

Sí, una habitación doble.
❷ Do you accept pets?

Sí. ¿Cuántas noches?
❸ Three nights.

Son ciento cuarenta euros.
❹ Is breakfast included?

Sí. Aquí tiene la llave.
❺ Thank you very much.

3 At the hotel

❶ ¿Tiene habitaciones libres?
tyenay abeeta-thyones leebres

❷ ¿Aceptan animales de compañía?
atheptan aneemales day kompanyeeah

❸ Tres noches.
tres noches

❹ ¿El desayuno está incluido?
el desayoonoh estah inklooeedoh

❺ Muchas gracias.
moochas grathyas

4 Negatives (5 minutes)

Make these sentences negative using the verb in brackets.

❶ Yo _____ hijos. (tener)

❷ Ellos _____ a Madrid mañana. (ir)

❸ Él _____ un café. (querer)

❹ Yo _____ el metro. (coger)

❺ La vista _____ muy bonita. (ser)

4 Negatives

❶ no tengo
noh tengoh

❷ no van
noh ban

❸ no quiere
noh kyairay

❹ no cojo
noh kohoh

❺ no es
no es

❺ toilets

❻ caravan

DE COMPRAS
Shopping

1 Warm up (1 minute)

Ask "How do I get to the station?" (pp.50-1)

Say "Turn left at the traffic lights" and "The station is opposite the café". (pp.50-1)

Small, traditional shops are still very common in Spain. But you can also find big supermarkets and shopping centres on the outskirts of cities. Local markets selling fresh, local produce can be found everywhere. Find out the market day from the **oficina de información turística** (*tourist office*).

2 Match and repeat (5 minutes)

Match the shops numbered 1 to 9 below and right to the Spanish in the panel. Then test yourself using the cover flap.

❶ **la panadería**
   lah panadaireeah

❷ **la pastelería**
   lah pastaylaireeah

❸ **el estanco**
   el estankoh

❹ **la carnicería**
   lah karnee-thaireeah

❺ **la charcutería**
   lah charkoo-taireeah

❻ **la librería**
   lah leebraireeah

❼ **la pescadería**
   lah peskadaireeah

❽ **la joyería**
   la hoyereeah

❾ **el banco**
   el bankoh

❶ baker

❷ cake shop

❹ butcher

❺ delicatessen

❼ fishmonger

❽ jeweller

Conversational tip If you want an everyday bar of soap or a tube of toothpaste, you need to go to a **droguería** (*drugstore*) rather than the **farmacia** (*pharmacy*). The **estanco** (*tobacconist*) is the place for all sorts of tobacco products and stamps. **Papelerías** cater for all your stationery needs. Most Spanish shops offer a free gift-wrapping service; you only need to ask: "**¿Me lo envuelve para regalo?**" (*May I have it gift-wrapped?*).

¿Dónde está la floristería?
donday estah lah floreestaireeah
Where is the florist?

❸ tobacconist

❻ bookshop

❾ bank

5 Say it (2 minutes)

Where is the bank?

Do you sell cheese?

Where do I pay?

3 Words to remember (4 minutes)

Familiarize yourself with these words and test yourself using the cover flap.

hardware shop	**la ferretería** _lah ferretaireeah_
antique shop	**el anticuario** _el anteekwareeoh_
hairdresser	**la peluquería** _lah pelookaireeah_
greengrocer	**la verdulería** _lah berdoolaireeah_
post office	**la oficina de correos** _lah ofeetheenah day korrayos_
shoe shop	**la zapatería** _lah thapataireeah_
dry cleaner	**la tintorería** _lah teentoraireeah_
grocer	**el ultramarinos** _el ooltramareenos_

4 Useful phrases (3 minutes)

Familiarize yourself with these phrases.

Where is the hairdresser?	**¿Dónde está la peluquería?** _donday estah lah pelookaireeah_
Where do I pay?	**¿Dónde se paga?** _donday say pagah_
I'm just looking, thank you.	**Sólo estoy mirando, gracias.** _soloh estoy meerandoh grathyas_
Do you sell phonecards?	**¿Tiene tarjetas telefónicas?** _tyenay tarhetas telefoneekas_
May I have two of those?	**¿Me pone dos de éstos?** _may ponay dos day estos_
Can I place an order?	**¿Puedo hacer un pedido?** _pwedoh ahther oon pedeedoh_

EN EL MERCADO
At the market

Warm up (1 minute)

What is Spanish for "40", "56", "77", "82", and "94"? (pp.10-11 and pp.30-1)

Say "I'd like a big room". (pp.64-5)

Ask "Do you have a small car?" (pp.64-5)

Spain uses the metric system of weights and measures. You need to ask for the produce in kilogrammes or grammes. Some larger items, such as melons or pineapples, tend to be sold as **la pieza** (as single items); other items, such as lettuce, may be sold in lots of two or three.

Match and repeat (4 minutes)

Match the numbered items in this scene with the text in the panel.

1 los tomates
   los tomates

2 las judías
   las hoodeeas

3 los champiñones
   los champeenyones

4 las uvas
   las oobas

5 los pepinos
   los pepeenos

6 las alcachofas
   las alkachofas

7 los guisantes
   los gheesantes

8 los pimientos
   los peemyaintos

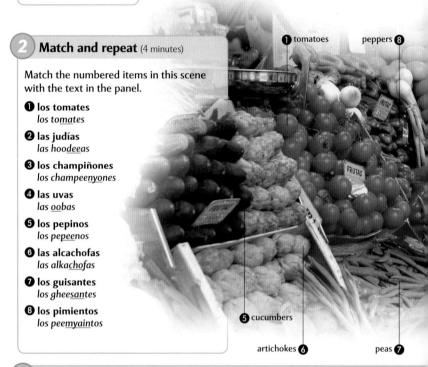

1 tomatoes   peppers **8**

5 cucumbers

artichokes **6**   peas **7**

In conversation: (3 minutes)

Quisiera tomates.
keesyairah tomates

I'd like some tomatoes.

¿De los grandes o de los pequeños?
day los grandes oh day los pekenyos

The large ones or the small ones?

Dos kilos de los pequeños, por favor.
dos keelos day los pekenyos, por fabor

Two kilos of the small ones, please.

Cultural tip Spain uses the common European currency, the euro, which is divided into 100 **centimos**. Spanish-speaking countries in Central and South America all have their own currencies. Argentina, Chile, Uruguay, Colombia, and México all call their currency the **peso**, which is divided into 100 **centavos**.

grapes ❹
mushrooms ❸
beans ❷

4 Useful phrases (5 minutes)

Practise these phrases and then test yourself using the cover flap.

Esa salchicha es demasiado cara.
ehsah salcheechah es demasyahdoh karah

That sausage is too expensive.

¿A cuánto está esa?
ah kwantoh estah ehsa

How much is that one?

5 Say it (2 minutes)

Two kilos of peas, please.

The mushrooms are too expensive.

How much are the grapes?

Eso es todo.
ehsoh es todoh

That'll be all.

¿Algo más, señorita?
algoh mas, senyoreetah

Anything else, miss?

Eso es todo, gracias. ¿Cuánto es?
ehsoh es todoh, grathyas. kwantoh es

That'll be all, thank you. How much?

Tres cincuenta.
tres theenkwentah

Three fifty.

What are these items
you could buy in a
supermarket? (pp.24–5)

la carne
el pescado
el queso
el zumo
el vino
el agua

EN EL
SUPERMERCADO
At the supermarket

Prices in supermarkets are usually lower than
in smaller shops. They offer all kinds of products,
with the larger out-of-town **hipermercados**
offering clothes, household goods, garden
furniture, and DIY products.

2 **Match and repeat** (5 minutes)

Look at the numbered product categories
and match them to the Spanish words in
the panel on the left.

**❶ los productos del
   hogar**
   los pro<u>dook</u>tos del oh<u>gar</u>

❷ la fruta
   lah <u>froo</u>tah

❸ las bebidas
   las be<u>bee</u>das

❹ los platos preparados
   los <u>pla</u>tos prepa<u>ra</u>dos

**❺ los productos de
   belleza**
   *los pro<u>dook</u>tos day
   be<u>ye</u>thah*

❻ los productos lácteos
   los pro<u>dook</u>tos <u>lak</u>teh-os

❼ la verdura
   lah ber<u>doo</u>rah

❽ los congelados
   los konhe<u>la</u>dos

household ❶
fruit ❷
drinks ❸
ready meals ❹

vegetables ❼
frozen foods ❽

Cultural tip You cannot usually take unweighed fruit
and vegetables sold by the kilo straight to the check-out
at a supermarket. There is usually a separate counter or
a self-service weighing machine.

3 Useful phrases (3 minutes)

Learn these phrases and then test yourself using the cover flap.

May I have a bag, please?	**¿Me da una bolsa, por favor?** *may dah oonah bolsah, por fabor*
Where are the drinks?	**¿Dónde están las bebidas?** *donday estan las bebeedas*
Where is the check-out, please?	**¿Dónde está la caja, por favor?** *donday estah lah kahah, por fabor*
Please key in your PIN.	**Por favor, meta su PIN.** *por fabor, metah soo peen*

❺ beauty products

❻ dairy products

4 Words to remember (4 minutes)

Learn these words and then test yourself using the cover flap.

bread	**el pan** *el pan*
milk	**la leche** *lah lechay*
butter	**la mantequilla** *lah mantekeeyah*
ham	**el jamón** *el hamon*
salt	**la sal** *lah sal*
pepper	**la pimienta** *lah peemyaintah*
washing powder	**el jabón de lavadora** *el habon day labadorah*
toilet paper	**el papel higiénico** *el papel eehyaineekoh*
nappies	**los pañales** *los panyales*

5 Say it (2 minutes)

Where are the dairy products?

May I have some cheese, please?

Where are the frozen foods?

LA ROPA Y LOS ZAPATOS
Clothes and shoes

1 Warm up (1 minute)

Say "I'd like...". (pp.22-3)

Ask "Do you have...?" (pp.14-15)

Say "38", "42", and "46". (pp.10-11 and pp.30-1)

Say "big", "small", "bigger", and "smaller". (pp.64-5)

Clothes and shoes are measured in metric sizes from 36 upwards. Even allowing for conversion of sizes, Spanish clothes tend to be cut smaller than English ones. Clothes size is **la talla**, but shoe size is **el número**.

2 Match and repeat (3 minutes)

Match the numbered items of clothing to the Spanish words in the panel on the left. Test yourself using the cover flap.

shirt **1**

tie **2**

jacket **3**

pocket **4**

sleeve **5**

trousers **6**

1 la camisa
lah kameesah

2 la corbata
lah korbatah

3 la chaqueta
lah chaketah

4 el bolsillo
el bolseeyoh

5 la manga
lah mangah

6 el pantalón
el pantalon

7 la falda
lah faldah

8 las medias
las medyas

9 los zapatos
los thapatos

Cultural tip As in most of mainland Europe, Spain uses the continental system of sizes. Women's clothes sizes usually range from 36 (UK 8, US 6) through to 46 (UK 20, US 18), and shoe sizes from 37 (UK 4, US 5½) to 45 (UK 11, US 12). For men's shirts, a size 41 is a 16-inch collar, 43 is a 17-inch collar, and 45 is an 18-inch collar.

3 Useful phrases (5 minutes)

Practise these phrases and then test yourself using the cover flap.

Do you have a larger size?	**¿Tiene una talla más grande?** *tyenay oonah tayah mas granday*
It's not what I want.	**No es lo que quiero.** *noh es loh kay kyairoh*
I'll take the pink one.	**Me quedo con el rosa.** *may kedoh kon el rrosah*

4 Words to remember (4 minutes)

Colours are adjectives (pp.64-5) and in most cases have a masculine and a feminine form. The feminine is usually formed by substituting an **a** for the final **o**.

red	**rojo/roja** *rrohoh/rrohah*
white	**blanco/blanca** *blankoh/blankah*
blue	**azul** *athool*
yellow	**amarillo/amarilla** *amareeyoh/amareeyah*
green	**verde** *berday*
black	**negro/negra** *negroh/negrah*

7 skirt

8 tights

9 shoes

5 Say it (2 minutes)

What shoe size?

Do you have a black jacket?

Do you have size 38?

Do you have a smaller size?

Respuestas
Answers (Cover with flap)

REPASE Y REPITA
Review and repeat

1 Market

❶ las alcachofas
las alkachofas

❷ los tomates
los tomates

❸ los guisantes
los gheesantes

❹ los pimientos
los peemyaintos

❺ las judías
las hoodeeas

1 Market (3 minutes)

Name the numbered vegetables in Spanish.

❶ artichokes ❷ tomatoes ❸ peas ❹ peppers beans ❺

2 Description

❶ The shoes are too expensive.

❷ My room is very small.

❸ I need a softer bed.

2 Description (2 minutes)

What do these sentences mean?

❶ Los zapatos son demasiados caros.

❷ Mi habitación es muy pequeña.

❸ Necesito una cama más blanda.

3 Shops

❶ la panadería
lah panadaireeah

❷ la joyería
lah hoyehreeah

❸ la librería
lah leebraireeah

❹ la pescadería
lah peskadaireeah

❺ la pastelería
lah pastaylaireeah

❻ la carnicería
lah karneethaireeah

3 Shops (3 minutes)

Name the numbered shops in Spanish. Then check your answers.

❶ baker

❷ jeweller

❸ bookshop

❹ fishmonger

❺ cake shop

❻ butcher

4 Supermarket (3 minutes)

What is the Spanish for the numbered product categories?

1 household products

2 beauty products

3 drinks

4 dairy products

5 frozen foods

4 Supermarket

1 **los productos del hogar**
los prodooktos del ohgar

2 **los productos de belleza**
los prodooktos day beyethah

3 **las bebidas**
las bebeedas

4 **los productos lácteos**
los prodooktos lakteh-os

5 **la verdura**
lah berdoorah

5 Museum (4 minutes)

Follow this conversation, replying in Spanish following the English prompts.

Buenos días. ¿Qué desean?
1 I'd like five tickets.

Son setenta y cinco euros.
2 That's very expensive!

No hacemos descuentos a los niños.
3 How much is a guide?

Quince euros.
4 Good. And five tickets, please.

Noventa euros, por favor.
5 Here you are. Where are the toilets?

A la derecha.
6 Thank you very much.

5 Museum

1 **Quisiera cinco entradas.**
keesyairah theenkoh entradas

2 **¡Es muy caro!**
es mwee karoh

3 **¿Cuánto cuesta una guía?**
kwantoh kwestah oonah gheeah

4 **Bien. Y cinco entradas, por favor.**
Byen. ee theenkoh entradas, por fabor

5 **Aquí tiene. ¿Dónde están los servicios?**
ahkee tyenay. donday estan los serbeethyos

6 **Muchas gracias.**
moochas grathyas

LAS OCUPACIONES
Jobs

Say "from which platform?" (pp.38–9)

What is the Spanish for the following family members: sister, brother, mother, father, son, and daughter? (pp.10-11)

Some occupations have commonly used feminine alternatives - for example, **enfermero** (*male nurse*) and **enfermera** (*female nurse*). Others remain the same. When you describe your occupation, you don't use **un/una** (*a*), saying simply **soy abogado** (*I'm a lawyer*), for example.

2 Words to remember: jobs (7 minutes)

Familiarize yourself with these words and test yourself using the cover flap. The feminine alternative is also shown.

médico *medeekoh*	doctor
dentista *denteestah*	dentist
enfermero/-a *enfermairoh/-ah*	nurse
profesor/-sora *profaysor/-sorah*	teacher
abogado/-a *abogadoh/-ah*	lawyer
contable *kontablay*	accountant
diseñador/-dora *deesenyador/-dorah*	designer
consultor/-a *konsooltor/-ah*	consultant
secretari0/-a *sekraytareeoh(-ah)*	secretary
comerciante *komerthyantay*	shopkeeper
electricista *elektreetheestah*	electrician
fontanero/-a *fontanairoh/-ah*	plumber
cocinero/-a *kotheenairoh/-ah*	cook/chef
albañil *albanyeel*	builder
autónomo/-a *aootohnomoh/-ah*	self-employed

Soy fontanero.
soy fontanairoh
I'm a plumber.

Es estudiante.
es estoodyantay
She is a student.

3 Put into practice (4 minutes)

Join in this conversation. Read the Spanish on the left and follow the instructions to form your reply. Then test yourself.

¿Cuál es su profesión?
kwal es soo profesyon

What do you do?

Say: I am a consultant.

Soy consultor.
soy konsooltor

¿Para qué empresa trabaja?
parah kay empresah trabahah

What company do you work for?

Say: I'm self-employed.

Soy autónomo.
soy aootohnomoh

¡Qué interesante!
kay intairaysantay

How interesting!

Say: And what is your profession?

¿Y cuál es su profesión?
ee kwal es soo profesyon

Soy dentista.
soy denteestah

I'm a dentist.

Say: My sister is a dentist too.

Mi hermana es dentista también.
mee airrmanah es denteestah tambyen

4 Words to remember: workplace (3 minutes)

La oficina central está en Madrid.
lah ofeetheenah thentral estah en madreed
Head office is in Madrid.

Familiarize yourself with these words and test yourself.

branch	**la sucursal** *lah sookoorsal*
department	**el departamento** *el departamaintoh*
manager	**el jefe** *el hefay*
employee	**el empleado** *el emplay-ahdoh*
reception	**la recepción** *lah rrethepthyon*
trainee	**el aprendiz** *el ahprendeeth*

LA OFICINA
The office

1 Warm up (1 minute)

Practise different ways of introducing yourself in different situations (pp.8-9). Mention your name, occupation (pp. 78-9), and any other information you'd like to volunteer.

An office environment or business situation has its own vocabulary in any language, but there are many items that are virtually universal. Be aware that Spanish computer keyboards have a different layout to the standard English QWERTY convention; they also include **ñ**, vowels with accents, **¡**, and **¿**.

2 Words to remember (5 minutes)

Familiarize yourself with these words. Read them aloud several times and try to memorize them. Conceal the Spanish with the cover flap and test yourself.

el monitor *el moneetor*	monitor
el ratón *el rraton*	mouse
el correo electrónico *el korrayoh elektroneekoh*	email
el internet *el eenternet*	internet
la contraseña *lah kontrasenyah*	password
la mensajería de voz *lah mensahereeah day both*	voicemail
el fax *el fax*	fax machine
la fotocopiadora *lah fotokopyadorah*	photocopier
la agenda *lah ah-hendah*	diary
la tarjeta de visita *lah tarhetah day beeseetah*	business card
la reunión *lah reh-oonyon*	meeting
la conferencia *lah konfairentheeah*	conference
el orden del día *el orden del deeah*	agenda

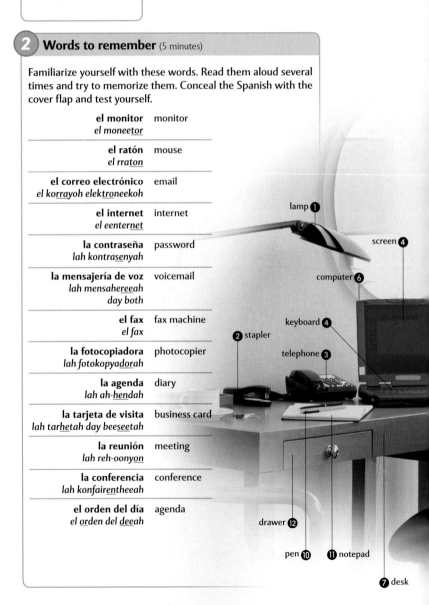

lamp **1**
screen **4**
computer **6**
keyboard **4**
2 stapler
telephone **3**
drawer **12**
pen **10**   **11** notepad
7 desk

3 Useful phrases (2 minutes)

Learn these phrases and then test yourself using the cover flap.

I need to make some photocopies.	**Necesito hacer unas fotocopias.** *netheseetoh ahther oonas fotokopyas*
I'd like to arrange an appointment.	**Quisiera organizar una cita.** *keesyairah organeethar oonah theetah*
I want to send an email.	**Quiero mandar un correo electrónico.** *kyairoh mandar oon korrayoh elektroneekoh*

4 Match and repeat (5 minutes)

Match the numbered items to the Spanish words on the left.

❶ **la lámpara** *lah lamparah*

❷ **la grapadora** *lah grapadohrah*

❸ **el teléfono** *el telefonoh*

❹ **la pantalla** *lah pantayah*

❺ **el teclado** *el tekladoh*

❻ **el ordenador** *el ordenador*

❼ **la mesa de escritorio** *lah mesah day eskreetoryoh*

❽ **el reloj** *el rrelokh*

❾ **la impresora** *lah impresorah*

❿ **el bolígrafo** *el boleegrafoh*

⓫ **el bloc** *el blok*

⓬ **el cajón** *el kahon*

⓭ **la silla giratoria** *lah seeyah heeratoreeah*

5 Say it (2 minutes)

I'd like to arrange a conference.

I need to send a fax.

Do you have email?

clock ❽

printer ❾

⓭ swivel chair

EL MUNDO ACADÉMICO
Academic world

In Spain, students are selected for a first degree (**una licenciatura**) by an average of secondary school grades and an exam. After graduation, some students go on to **un máster** (master's degree) or **un doctora do** (PhD).

2 **Useful phrases** (3 minutes)

Practise these phrases and then test yourself using the cover flap.

¿Cuál es su especialidad?
kwal es soo espetheeahleedad
What is your field?

Hago investigación en bioquímica.
ahgoh inbesteegathyon en beeohkeemeekah
I am doing research in biochemistry.

Soy licenciado en derecho.
soy leethentheeahdoh en derechoh
I have a degree in law.

Voy a dar una conferencia sobre arquitectura.
boy ah dar oonah konfairayntheeah sobreh arkeetektoorah
I'm going to give a lecture on architecture.

3 **In conversation** (5 minutes)

Hola, soy la profesora Fernández.
o-lah, soy lah profaysorah fernandeth

Hello, I'm Professor Fernandez.

¿De qué universidad es usted?
deh keh ooneeberseedad es oosted

What university are you from?

De la Universidad de Murcia.
deh lah ooneeberseedad deh moortheeah

From the University of Murcia.

4 Words to remember (4 minutes)

Familiarize yourself with these words and then test yourself.

Tenemos un stand en la feria.
tenemos oon estand en la fereeah
We have a stand at the trade fair.

conference/lecture	**la conferencia** *lah konfairaintheeah*
trade fair	**la feria** *lah fereeah*
seminar	**el seminario** *el semeenaryoh*
lecture theatre	**el anfiteatro** *el anfeetay-ahtroh*
conference room	**la sala de conferencias** *lah sahlah deh konferaintheeas*
exhibition	**la exposición** *lah eksposeethyon*
library	**la biblioteca** *lah bibleeotekah*
university lecturer	**el profesor de universidad** *el profaysor deh ooneeberseedad*
professor	**el catedrático** *el katedrateekoh*
medicine	**medicina** *medeetheenah*
science	**ciencias** *thyaintheeas*
literature	**literatura** *leetairatoorah*
engineering	**ingeniería** *inhainyaireeah*

5 Say it (2 minutes)

I'm doing research in medicine.

I have a degree in literature.

She's the professor.

¿Cuál es su especialidad?
kwal es soo espethyaleedad

What's your field?

Hago investigación en ingeniería.
ahgoh inbesteegathyon en inhenyaireeah

I'm doing research in engineering.

¡Qué interesante! Yo también.
keh intairaysantay. yoh tambeeayn

How interesting! Me too.

LOS NEGOCIOS
In business

1 Warm up (1 minute)

Ask "Can I ...?" (pp.34-5)

Say "I want to send an email". (pp.80-1)

Say "I'd like to arrange an appointment". (pp.80-1)

You will receive a more friendly reception and make a good impression if you make the effort to begin a meeting with a short introduction in Spanish, even if your vocabulary is limited. After that, all parties will probably be happy to continue the proceedings in English.

2 Words to remember (6 minutes)

Familiarize yourself with these words and then test yourself by concealing the Spanish with the cover flap.

el programa *el programah*	schedule
la entrega *lah entraygah*	delivery
el pago *el pahgoh*	payment
el presupuesto *el praysoopwestoh*	budget/estimate
el precio *el praythyoh*	price
el documento *el dokoomentoh*	document
la factura *lah faktoorah*	invoice
la propuesta *lah propwestah*	proposal
los beneficios *los baynayfeethyos*	profits
las ventas *las bentas*	sales
los números *los noomeros*	figures

el cliente
el klyaintay
client

el informe
el informay
report

Cultural tip A long lunch with wine is still a regular feature of doing business in Spain. As a visiting client you can expect to be taken out to a restaurant, and as a supplier you should consider entertaining your business customers.

3 Useful phrases (6 minutes)

Practise these useful business phrases and then test yourself using the cover flap.

¿Firmamos el contrato?
feermamos el kontratoh
Shall we sign the contract?

el ejecutivo
el eh-hekooteeboh
executive

Me manda el contrato, por favor.
may mandah el kontratoh, por fabor

Please send me the contract.

¿Hemos acordado un programa?
ehmos akordadoh oon programah

Have we agreed a schedule?

el contrato
el kontratoh
contract

¿Cuándo puede hacer la entrega?
kwandoh pweday ahther lah entregah

When can you make the delivery?

¿Cuál es el presupuesto?
kwal es el praysoopwestoh

What's the budget?

4 Say it (2 minutes)

Can you send me the estimate?

Have we agreed a price?

What are the profits?

¿Me puede mandar la factura?
may pweday mandar lah faktoorah

Can you send me the invoice?

REPASE Y REPITA
Review and repeat

Respuestas
Answers (Cover with flap)

1 At the office

❶ **la grapadora**
lah grapadorah

❷ **la lámpara**
lah lamparah

❸ **el ordenador**
el ordenador

❹ **el bolígrafo**
el boleegrafoh

❺ **el reloj**
el rrelokh

❻ **el bloc**
el blok

❼ **la mesa de escritorio**
lah mesah day eskreetoryoh

1 At the office (4 minutes)

Name these items.

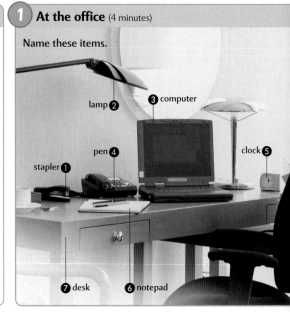

lamp ❷
❸ computer
pen ❹
clock ❺
stapler ❶
❼ desk
❻ notepad

2 Jobs

❶ **médico**
medeekoh

❷ **fontanero/-a**
fontanairoh/-ah

❸ **comerciante**
komerthyantay

❹ **contable**
kontablay

❺ **estudiante**
estoodyantay

❻ **abogado/-a**
abogadoh/-ah

2 Jobs (3 minutes)

What are these jobs in Spanish?

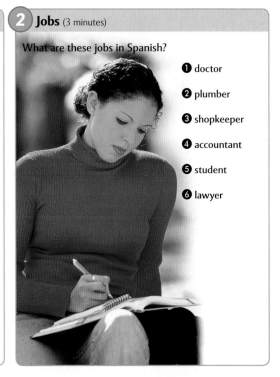

❶ doctor
❷ plumber
❸ shopkeeper
❹ accountant
❺ student
❻ lawyer

3 Work (4 minutes)

Answer these questions following the English prompts.

¿Para qué empresa trabaja?
❶ Say: I am self-employed.

¿En qué universidad está?
❷ Say: I'm at the University of Salamanca.

¿Cuál es su especialidad?
❸ Say: I'm doing research in medicine.

¿Hemos acordado un programa?
❹ Say: Yes, my secretary has the schedule.

3 Work

❶ **Soy autónomo.**
soy aootonomoh

❷ **Estoy en la Universidad de Salamanca.**
estoy en lah ooneeberseedad day salamankah

❸ **Hago investigación en medicina.**
ahgoh inbesteegathyon en medeetheenah

❹ **Sí. mi secretaria tiene el programa.**
see. mee sekretareeah tyenay el programah

4 How much? (4 minutes)

Answer the question with the amount shown in brackets.

❶ ¿Cuánto cuesta el desayuno? (€3.50)

❷ ¿Cuánto cuesta la habitación? (€47)

❸ ¿Cuánto cuesta un kilo de tomates? (€3.25)

❹ ¿Cuánto cuesta un plaza para cuatro noches? (€60)

4 How much?

❶ **Son tres euros cincuenta.**
son tres eh-ooros theenkwentah

❷ **Son cuarenta y siete euros.**
son kwarentah ee seeaytay eh-ooros

❸ **Son tres euros veinticinco.**
son tres eh-ooros beynteetheenkoh

❹ **Son sesenta euros.**
son sesentah eh-ooros

EN LA FARMACIA
At the chemist

1 Warm up (1 minute)

Say "I'm allergic to nuts". (pp.24-5)

Say the verb "tener" (to have) in all its forms: yo, tú, él/ella, nosotros(-as), vosotros(-as), ellos (-as). (pp.14-15)

Spanish pharmacists are qualified to give advice and sell over-the-counter medicines, as well as dispense prescription medicines. There is generally a **farmacia de guardia** (*duty pharmacy*) to provide 24-hour service in every town – a list is displayed in every pharmacy.

2 Match and repeat (3 minutes)

Match the numbered items to the Spanish words in the panel on the left and test yourself using the cover flap.

1 la venda
lah bendah

2 el jarabe
el harabay

3 las gotas
las gotas

4 la tirita
lah teereetah

5 la jeringuilla
lah hereengheeyah

6 la crema
lah kremah

7 el supositorio
el sooposeetoryoh

8 la pastilla
lah pasteeyah

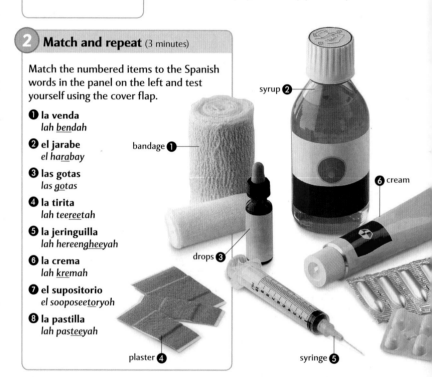

syrup **2**
bandage **1**
6 cream
drops **3**
plaster **4**
syringe **5**

3 In conversation (3 minutes)

Buenos días, señor. ¿Qué desea?
bwenos deeyas, senyor. kay desayah

Good morning, sir. What would you like?

Tengo dolor de estómago.
tengoh dolor day estomagoh

I have a stomach ache.

¿Tiene diarrea?
tyenay deeahrrayah

Do you have diarrhoea?

4 Words to remember (2 minutes)

Familiarize yourself with these words and test yourself using the cover flap.

Tengo dolor de cabeza.
tengoh dolor day kabethah

I have a headache.

headache	**el dolor de cabeza** _el dolor day kabethah_
stomach ache	**el dolor de estómago** _el dolor day estomagoh_
diarrhoea	**la diarrea** _lah deeahrrayah_
cold	**el resfriado** _el rresfreeahdoh_
cough	**la tos** _lah tos_
sunstroke	**la insolación** _lah eensolatheeyon_
toothache	**el dolor de muelas** _el dolor day mwelas_

6 Say it (2 minutes)

I have a cold.

Do you have that as a cream?

He has toothache.

❼ suppository

❽ tablet

5 Useful phrases (4 minutes)

Practise these phrases and then test yourself using the cover flap.

I have sunstroke.	**Tengo una insolación.** _tengoh oonah eensolatheeyon_
Do you have that as a syrup?	**¿Lo tiene en jarabe?** _loh tyenay en harabay_
I'm allergic to penicillin.	**Soy alérgico a la penicilina.** _soy alerheekoh ah lah peneetheeleenah_

No, pero tengo dolor de cabeza.
noh, peroh tengoh dolor day kabethah

No, but I have a headache.

Aquí tiene.
ahkee tyenay

Here you are.

¿Lo tiene en pastilla?
loh tyenay en pasteeyah

Do you have this as pills?

1 **Warm up** (1 minute)

Say "I have a toothache" and "I have a sunstroke". (pp.88-9)

Say the Spanish for "red", "green", "black", and "yellow". (pp.74-5)

EL CUERPO
The body

You are most likely to need to refer to parts of the body in the context of illness - for example, when describing aches and pains to a doctor. The most common phrases for talking about discomfort are **Tengo un dolor en la/el...** (*I have a pain in the...*) and **Me duele la/el...** (*My ... hurts me*).

2 **Match and repeat: body** (6 minutes)

Match the numbered parts of the body with the list on the left. Test yourself by using the cover flap.

1 **la mano**
lah manoh

2 **la cabeza**
lah kabethah

3 **el hombro**
el ombroh

4 **el codo**
el kodoh

5 **el pelo**
el peloh

6 **el brazo**
el brathoh

7 **el cuello**
el kweyoh

8 **el pecho**
el pechoh

9 **el estómago**
el estomagoh

10 **la pierna**
lah pyairnah

11 **la rodilla**
lah rrodeeyah

12 **el pie**
el pee-ay

- **1** hand
- **4** elbow
- **5** hair
- **2** head
- **6** arm
- **3** shoulder
- **7** neck
- **8** chest
- **9** stomach
- **10** leg
- **11** knee
- **12** foot

3 Match and repeat: face (3 minutes)

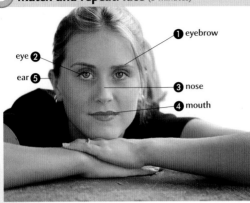

1 eyebrow

eye **2**

ear **5**

3 nose

4 mouth

Match the numbered facial features with the list on the right.

1 la ceja
lah thayah

2 el ojo
el oh-hoh

3 la nariz
lah nareeth

4 la boca
lah bokah

5 la oreja
lah ohrayah

4 Useful phrases (3 minutes)

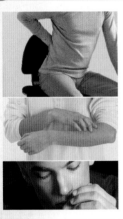

Learn these phrases and then test yourself using the cover flap.

I have a pain in my back.	**Tengo un dolor en la espalda.** *tengoh oon dolor en lah espalda*
I have a rash on my arm.	**Tengo un sarpullido en el brazo.** *tengoh oon sarpooyeedoh en el brathoh*
I don't feel well.	**No me encuentro bien.** *noh may enkwentroh byen*

5 Put into practice (2 minutes)

Join in this conversation and test yourself using the cover flap.

¿Cuál es el problema?
kwal es el problemah

What's the problem?

Say: I don't feel well.

No me encuentro bien.
noh may enkwentroh byen

¿Dónde le duele?
donday lay dwelay

Where does it hurt?

Say: I have a pain in the shoulder.

Tengo un dolor en el hombro.
tengoh oon dolor en el ombroh

EN EL MÉDICO
At the doctor

1 Warm up (1 minute)

Say "I need some tablets". (pp.60-1, pp.88-9)

Say "He needs some cream". (pp.88-9)

What is the Spanish for "I don't have a son". (pp.10-15)

Unless it's an emergency, you have to book an appointment with the doctor and pay when you leave. You can usually reclaim the money if you have medical insurance. Your hotel, a local pharmacy, or a tourist information office may be able to tell you the names and addresses of local doctors.

2 Useful phrases you may hear (3 minutes)

Practise these phrases and then test yourself using the cover flap to conceal the Spanish on the left.

No es grave. *noh es gravay*	It's not serious.
Necesita hacerse unas pruebas. *netheseetah ahthersay oonas prwaybas*	You need to have some tests.
Tiene una infección de riñón. *tyenay oonah infekthyon day rreenyon*	You have a kidney infection.
Necesita ir al hospital. *netheseetah eer al ospeetal*	You need to go to hospital.

Le voy a dar una receta.
lay boy ah dar oonah rrethetah
I'm going to give you a prescription.

3 In conversation (5 minutes)

¿Cuál es el problema?
kwal es el problemah

What's the problem?

Tengo un dolor en el pecho.
tengoh oon dolor en el pechoh

I have a pain in my chest.

Déjeme que la examine.
dayhaymay kay lah eksameenay

Let me examine you.

4 Useful phrases you may need to say (4 minutes)

Estoy embarazada.
estoy embarathadah
I am pregnant.

Practise these phrases and then test yourself using the cover flap.

I am diabetic.	**Soy diabético/-a.** *soy deeahbeteekoh/-ah*
I am epileptic.	**Soy epiléptico/-a.** *soy epeelepteekoh/-ah*
I'm asthmatic.	**Soy asmático/-a.** *soy asmateekoh/-ah*
I have a heart condition.	**Tengo un problema de corazón.** *tengoh oon problemah day korathon*
I have a temperature.	**Tengo fiebre.** *tengoh fyaybray*
I feel faint.	**Estoy mareado.** *estoy maray-ahdoh*
It's urgent.	**Es urgente.** *es oorhentay*

Conversational tip

If you are an EU national, you are entitled to free emergency medical treatment in Spain on production of a European Health Insurance Card or an E111 form. For an ambulance, call 112.

5 Say it (2 minutes)

My son is diabetic.

I have a pain in my arm.

It's not urgent.

¿Es grave?
es gravay

Is it serious?

No, sólo tiene indigestión.
noh, soloh tyenay indeehestyon

No, you only have indigestion.

¡Menos mal!
maynos mal

What a relief!

EN EL HOSPITAL
At the hospital

1 **Warm up** (1 minute)

Say "How long is the journey?" (pp.42-3)

Ask "Is is serious?" (pp.92-3)

What is the Spanish for "mouth" and "head"? (pp.90-1)

It is useful to know a few basic phrases relating to hospitals and medical treatment for use in an emergency, or in case you need to visit a friend or colleague in hospital. Most Spanish hospitals have only two beds per room and their own en-suite bathroom facilities.

2 **Useful phrases** (5 minutes)

Familiarize yourself with these phrases. Conceal the Spanish with the cover flap and test yourself.

¿Cuáles son las horas de visita? _kwales son las oras day beeseetah_	What are the visiting hours?
¿Cuánto tiempo va a tardar? _kwantoh tyempoh bah ah tardar_	How long will it take?
¿Va a doler? _bah ah doler_	Will it hurt?
Túmbese aquí por favor. _toombesay ahkee por fabor_	Please lie down here.
No puede comer nada. _noh pweday komer nadah_	You cannot eat anything.
No mueva la cabeza. _noh mwebah lah kabethah_	Don't move your head.
Abra la boca por favor. _ahbrah lah bokah por fabor_	Please open your mouth.
Necesita un análisis de sangre. _netheseetah oon analeesees day sangray_	You need a blood test.

¿Se encuentra mejor? _say enkwentrah mehor_ Are you feeling better?

¿Dónde está la sala de espera? _donday estah lah salah day esperah_ Where is the waiting room?

el gotero _el goteroh_ drip

3 Words to remember (4 minutes)

Su radiografía es normal.
soo rradyografeeah es normal
Your x-ray is normal.

Familiarize yourself with these words and test yourself using the cover flap.

emergency department	**el servicio de urgencias** *el serbeethyoh day oorhentheeas*
x-ray department	**el servicio de radiología** *el serbeethyoh day rradyoloheeah*
children's ward	**la sala de pediatría** *lah salah day pedeeatreeah*
operating theatre	**el quirófano** *el keerofanoh*
waiting room	**la sala de espera** *lah salah day esperah*
stairs	**las escaleras** *las eskaleras*

4 Put into practice (3 minutes)

Join in this conversation. Cover up the text on the right and complete the anwering part of the dialogue in Spanish. Check your answers and repeat if necessary.

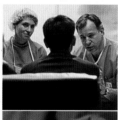

Tiene una infección.
tyenay oonah infekthyon

You have an infection.

Ask: Do I need tests?

¿Necesito hacerme pruebas?
netheseetoh ahthermay prwaybas

Primero necesita un análisis de sangre.
preemeroh netheseetah oon analeesees day sangray

First you will need a blood test.

Ask: Will it hurt?

¿Me va a doler?
may bah ah doler

5 Say it (2 minutes)

Does he need a blood test?

Where is the children's ward?

Do I need an x-ray?

No, no se preocupe.
noh, noh say pray-okoopay

No. Don't worry.

Ask: How long will it take?

¿Cuánto tiempo va a tardar?
kwantoh tyempoh bah ah tardar

REPASE Y REPITA
Review and repeat

Respuestas
Answers (Cover with flap)

1 The body

1 la cabeza
lah kabethah

2 el brazo
el brathoh

3 el pecho
el pechoh

4 el estómago
el estomagoh

5 la pierna
lah pyairnah

6 la rodilla
lah rrodeeyah

7 el pie
el pee-ay

1 The body (4 minutes)

Name the numbered body parts in Spanish.

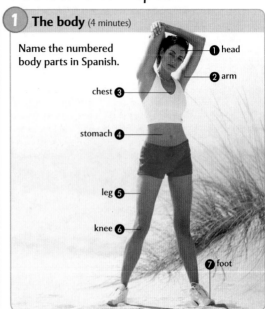

- **1** head
- **2** arm
- chest **3**
- stomach **4**
- leg **5**
- knee **6**
- **7** foot

2 On the phone

1 Quisiera hablar con Ana Flores.
keesyairah hablar kon anna flores

2 Luis Cortés de Don Frío.
looees kortes day don free-oh

3 ¿Puedo dejar un mensaje?
pwedoh dehar oon mensahay

4 La cita el lunes a las once está bien.
lah theetah el loones ah las onthay estah byen

5 Gracias, adiós.
grathyas, addy-os

2 On the phone (4 minutes)

You are arranging an appointment. Follow the conversation, replying in Spanish following the English prompts.

Dígame, Apex Finanzas.
1 I'd like to speak to Ana Flores.

¿De parte de quién?
2 Luis Cortés, of Don Frío.

Lo siento, está comunicando.
3 Can I leave a message?

Sí, dígame.
4 The appointment on Monday at 11am is fine.

Muy bien, adiós.
5 Thank you, goodbye.

3 Clothing (3 minutes)

Say the Spanish words for the numbered items of clothing.

tie ❶
jacket ❷
skirt ❹
trousers ❸
tights ❻
shoes ❺

3 Clothing

❶ **la corbata**
lah korbatah

❷ **la chaqueta**
lah chaketah

❸ **el pantalón**
el pantalon

❹ **la falda**
lah faldah

❺ **los zapatos**
los thapatos

❻ **las medias**
las medeeas

4 At the doctor's (4 minutes)

Say these phrases in Spanish.

❶ I don't feel well.
❷ I have a heart condition.
❸ Do I need to go to hospital?
❹ I am pregnant.

4 At the doctor's

❶ **No me encuentro bien.**
noh may enkwentroh byen

❷ **Tengo un problema de corazón.**
tengoh oon problemah day korathon

❸ **¿Necesito ir al hospital?**
netheseetoh eer al ospeetal

❹ **Estoy embarazada.**
estoy embarathadah

1 Warm up (1 minute)

Say the months of the year in Spanish. (pp.28-9)

Ask "Is there a car park?" and "Are there toilets?" (pp.48-9 and pp.62-3)

EN CASA
At home

Many city-dwellers live in apartment blocks (**edificios**), but in rural areas the houses tend to be detached (**chalet**). If you want to know how big it is you will need to ask in square metres. If you want to know how many bedrooms there are ask **¿Cuántos dormitorios hay?**.

2 Match and repeat (5 minutes)

Match the numbered items to the list and test yourself using the flap.

1 **la chimenea**
lah cheeme*nay*ah

2 **la ventana**
lah ben*tan*ah

3 **el tejado**
el te*had*oh

4 **la terraza**
lah te*rrat*ha

5 **la persiana**
lah perseee*an*ah

6 **el muro**
el *moor*oh

7 **la puerta**
lah *pwer*tah

8 **el garaje**
el *gar*ahay

chimney **1**   **2** window   roof **3**

shutters **5**

door **7**

wall **6**

Cultural tip You almost never see a Spanish home without shutters at every window. These are closed at night and often during the heat of the day in summer. Curtains, where they exist at all, tend to be more for decoration. Carpets are not popular in Spanish homes; ceramic tiles or parquet floors with rugs are a more common flooring solution.

3 Words to remember (4 minutes)

¿Cuánto es el alquiler al mes?
kwantoh es el alkeeler al mes
What is the rent per month?

Familiarize yourself with these words and
test yourself using the cover flap.

room	**la habitación**	*lah abeetathyon*
floor	**el suelo**	*el sweloh*
ceiling	**el techo**	*el techoh*
bedroom	**el dormitorio**	*el dormeetoreeoh*
bathroom	**el cuarto de baño**	*el kwartoh day banyoh*
kitchen	**la cocina**	*lah kotheenah*
dining room	**el comedor**	*el komedor*
living room	**el cuarto de estar**	*el kwartoh day estar*
cellar	**el sótano**	*el sotahnoh*
attic	**el ático**	*el ahteekoh*

terrace ❹

4 Put into practice (3 minutes)

Practise these phrases and test yourself.

¿Hay un garaje?
ah-ee oon garahay

Is there a garage?

garage ❽

¿Cuándo está disponible?
kwandoh estah deesponeeblay

When is it available?

5 Say it (2 minutes)

Is there a dining room?

Is it large?

Is it available in July?

¿Está amueblado?
estah amwebladoh

Is it furnished?

EN LA CASA
Inside the house

1 Warm up (1 minute)

What is the Spanish for "table", "chair", "toilet(s)", and "curtains"? (pp.20-1, pp.80-1, pp.52-3, pp.60-1)

Say "beautiful", "soft", and "big". (pp.64-5)

If you're renting a holiday house or villa in Spain, the most usual option is to take it for a full month or, if not, for a **quincena**, the first or last fifteen days of the month. You will need to check in advance whether the cost of utilities is included in the rent. Most holiday homes have no telephone.

2 Match and repeat (3 minutes)

Match the numbered items to the list in the panel on the left. Then test yourself by concealing the Spanish with the cover flap.

❶ **la encimera**
   lah entheemerah

❷ **el fregadero**
   el fregaderoh

❸ **el microondas**
   el meekro-ondas

❹ **el horno**
   el ornoh

❺ **la cocina**
   lah kotheenah

❻ **el frigorífico**
   el freegoreefeekoh

❼ **la mesa**
   lah mesah

❽ **la silla**
   lah seeyah

❺ cooker   ❶ worktop
❻ fridge
❽ chair
❹ oven   ❼ table

3 In conversation (3 minutes)

Este es el horno.
estay es el ornoh

This is the oven.

¿Hay también un lavavajillas?
ah-ee tambyen oon lababaheeyas

Is there a dishwasher as well?

Sí, y hay un congelador grande.
see, ee ah-ee oon konhelador granday

Yes, and there's a big freezer.

4 **Words to remember** (2 minutes)

Familiarize yourself with these words
and test yourself using the cover flap.

El sofá es nuevo.
el sofah es nweboh
The sofa is new.

➋ sink   microwave ➌

wardrobe	**el armario**	*el armaryoh*
sofa	**el sofá**	*el sofah*
fireplace	**la chimenea**	*lah cheemenayah*
carpet	**la moqueta**	*lah moketah*
bath	**la bañera**	*lah banyerah*
toilet	**el váter**	*el bater*
wash basin	**el lavabo**	*el lababoh*

5 **Useful phrases** (4 minutes)

Practise these phrases and then test yourself.

The cooker is broken.	**La cocina no funciona.** *lah kotheenah noh foonthyonah*
I don't like the curtains.	**No me gustan las cortinas.** *noh may goostan las korteenas*
Is electricity included?	**¿Está incluida la electricidad?** *estah eenklooeedah lah ehektreetheedad*

6 **Say it** (2 minutes)

Is there a microwave?

I like the fireplace.

What a soft sofa!

Todo está muy nuevo.
todoh estah mwee nweboh

Everything is very new.

Y aquí está la lavadora.
ee ahkee estah lah labadorah

And here's the
washing machine.

¡Qué azulejos más bonitos!
kay ah-thoolayhos mas boneetos

What beautiful tiles!

EL JARDÍN
The garden

Say "I need" and "you need". (pp.64-5, pp.92-4)

What is the Spanish for "day" and "month"? (pp.28-9)

Say the days of the week. (pp.28-9)

The garden of a house or a villa may be communal, or at least partly shared. Check with the estate agent or rental agent carefully to establish the position. In some cases, a charge for upkeep of the garden may be included with the rent of an apartment. Check with the agent.

2 **Words to remember** (3 minutes)

Familiarize yourself with these words and test yourself using the cover flap.

la máquina cortacésped *lah makeenah kortathesped*	lawn mower
la horca *lah orkah*	fork
la pala *lah palah*	spade
el rastrillo *el rrastreeyoh*	rake
el vivero *el beeberoh*	garden centre

terrace **1**

tree **2**

flowers **7**

soil **3**

weeds **8**

path **9**

3 **Useful phrases** (4 minutes)

Practise these phrases and then test yourself using the cover flap.

The gardener comes once a week.	**El jardinero viene una vez a la semana.** *el hardeenairoh byainay oonah beth ah lah semanah*
Can you mow the lawn?	**¿Puede cortar el césped?** *pweday kortar el thesped*
Is the garden private?	**¿Es el jardín privado?** *es el hardeen preebadoh*
The garden needs watering.	**El jardín necesita que lo rieguen.** *el hardeen netheseetah kay loh rreeayghen*

5 hedge
4 lawn

4 **Words to remember** (5 minutes)

Match the numbered items to the words in the panel on the right.

1 **la terraza** *lah terrathah*

2 **el árbol** *el arbol*

3 **la tierra** *lah tyairrah*

4 **el césped** *el thesped*

5 **el seto** *el setoh*

6 **las plantas** *las plantas*

7 **las flores** *las flores*

8 **las malas hierbas** *las malas yerbas*

9 **el camino** *el kameenoh*

10 **el parterre** *el partairray*

6 plants
10 flowerbed

5 **Say it** (2 minutes)

The lawn needs water.

Are there any trees?

The gardener comes on Fridays.

LOS ANIMALES DE COMPAÑÍA
Pets

1 **Warm up** (1 minute)

Say "My name's ...".
(pp.8-9)

Say "Don't worry".
(pp.94-5)

What's "your" in Spanish?
(pp.12-13)

"Pet passports" are now available to enable holiday-makers and commuters to take their pets with them to Spain and avoid quarantine on return to the UK. Consult your vet for details on the necessary vaccinations and paperwork.

2 **Match and repeat** (3 minutes)

Match the numbered animals to the Spanish words in the panel on the left. Then test yourself using the cover flap.

1 **el gato**
  el gatoh

2 **el conejo**
  el konehoh

3 **el pájaro**
  el paharoh

4 **el pez**
  el peth

5 **el perro**
  el perroh

6 **el hámster**
  el hamster

bird **3**
2 rabbit
dog **5**
1 cat

3 **Useful phrases** (4 minutes)

Learn these phrases and then test yourself using the cover flap.

¿Es bueno el perro? *es bwenoh el perroh*	Is this dog friendly?
¿Puedo llevar el perro? *pwedoh yebar el perroh*	Can I bring my dog?
Me dan miedo los gatos. *may dan myaydoh los gatos*	I'm frightened of cats.
Mi perro no muerde. *mee perroh noh mweday*	My dog doesn't bite.

Este gato está lleno de pulgas.
estay gatoh estah yenoh day poolgas
This cat is full of fleas.

Cultural tip Many dogs in Spain are working or guard dogs and you may encounter them tethered or roaming free. Approach farms and rural houses with particular care. Look out for warning notices such as **¡Cuidado con el perro!** (*Beware of the dog*).

¡CUIDADO CON EL PERRO!

4 Words to remember (4 minutes)

Familiarize yourself with these words and test yourself using the cover flap.

basket	**la cesta** *lah thestah*
cage	**la jaula** *lah haoolah*
bowl	**el bol** *el bol*
collar	**el collar** *el koyar*
lead	**la correa** *lah korray-ah*
vet	**el veterinario** *el betereenaryoh*
vaccination	**la vacuna** *lah bakoonah*
pet passport	**el pasaporte de animales** *el pasaportay* *day aneemales*
flea spray	**el spray antipulgas** *el espraee anteepoolgas*

Mi perro no está bien.
mee perroh noh estah byen
My dog is not well.

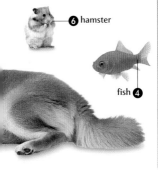

❻ hamster

fish ❹

5 Put into practice (3 minutes)

Join in this conversation. Read the Spanish on the left and follow the instructions to make your reply. Then test yourself by concealing the answers with the cover flap.

¿Es suyo este perro?
es sooyoh estay perroh

Is this your dog?

Say: Yes, he's called Sandy.

Sí, se llama Sandy.
see, say yamah Sandy

Me dan miedo los perros.
may dan myaydoh los perros

I'm frightened of dogs.

Say: Don't worry.
He's friendly.

No se preocupe.
Es bueno.
noh say prayohkoopay.
es bwenoh

REPASE Y REPITA
Review and repeat

1 Colours

❶ **negra**
negrah

❷ **pequeños**
pekenyos

❸ **rojo**
rrohoh

❹ **verde**
berday

❺ **amarillos**
amareeyos

1 Colours (4 minutes)

Complete the sentences with the Spanish word
for the colour in brackets. Watch out for masculine
and feminine.

❶ Quisiera la camisa _____. (black)

❷ Estos zapatos son muy _____. (small)

❸ ¿Tiene este traje en _____? (red)

❹ No, pero lo tengo en _____. (green)

❺ Quiero los zapatos _____. (yellow)

2 Kitchen

❶ **la cocina**
lah kotheenah

❷ **el frigorífico**
el freegoreefeekoh

❸ **el fregadero**
el fregaderoh

❹ **el microondas**
el meekro-ondas

❺ **el horno**
el ornoh

❻ **la silla**
lah seeyah

❼ **la mesa**
lah mesah

2 Kitchen (4 minutes)

Say the Spanish words for the numbered items.

cooker ❶   fridge ❷

❺ oven   chair ❻

Respuestas
Answers (Cover with flap)

3 House (4 minutes)

You are visiting a house in Spain. Join in the conversation, asking questions in Spanish following the English prompts.

Éste es el cuarto de estar.
❶ What a lovely fireplace.

Sí, y tiene una cocina muy grande.
❷ How many bedrooms are there?

Hay tres dormitorios.
❸ Do you have a garage?

Sí, pero no hay un jardín.
❹ When is it available?

En julio.
❺ What is the rent a month?

3 House

❶ **¡Qué chimenea más bonita!**
kay cheemenayah mas boneetah

❷ **¿Cuántos dormitorios hay?**
kwantos dormeetoreeos ah-ee

❸ **¿Tiene garaje?**
tyenay garahay

❹ **¿Cuándo está disponible?**
kwandoh estah deesponeeblay

❺ **¿Cuánto es el alquiler al mes?**
kwantoh es el alkeeler al mes

microwave ❹
❸ sink
table ❼

4 At home (3 minutes)

Say the Spanish for the following items.

❶ washing machine
❷ sofa
❸ attic
❹ dining room
❺ tree
❻ garden

4 At home

❶ **la lavadora**
lah labadorah

❷ **el sofá**
el sofah

❸ **el ático**
el ahteekoh

❹ **el comedor**
el komedor

❺ **el árbol**
el arbol

❻ **el jardín**
el hardeen

EL BANCO Y LA OFICINA DE CORREOS
Bank and post office

1 Warm up (1 minute)

Ask "How do I get to the bank?" and "How do I get to the post office?" (pp.50-1)

What's the Spanish for "passport"? (pp.54-5)

How do you ask "What time is the meeting?" (pp.30-1)

Banks and post offices usually open only until lunchtime (approximately 2pm) and are generally closed at weekends. **Cajas de ahorros** (*savings banks*) have different hours. In summer, operation times may be shorter.

2 Words to remember: post (3 minutes)

los sellos *los seyos*	stamps
la postal *lah postal*	postcard
el paquete *el paketay*	parcel
por avión *por abyon*	by air mail
el correo certificado *el korrayoh therteefeekadoh*	registered post
el buzón *el boothon*	post box
el código postal *el kodeegoh postal*	postcode
el cartero *el kartairoh*	postman

Familiarize yourself with these words and test yourself using the cover flap to conceal the Spanish on the left.

el sobre
el sobray
envelope

¿Cuánto es para el Reino Unido?
kwantoh es parah el rrayeenoh ooneedoh
How much is it for the United Kingdom?

3 In conversation (3 minutes)

Quisiera sacar dinero.
keesyairah sakar deeneroh

I'd like to withdraw some money.

¿Tiene identificación?
tyenay eedenteefeekathyon

Do you have any ID?

Sí, aquí tiene mi pasaporte.
see, ahkee tyenay mee pasaportay

Yes, here's my passport.

¿Cómo puedo pagar?
komoh pwedoh pagar
How can I pay?

4 Words to remember: bank (2 minutes)

Familiarize yourself with these words and test yourself
using the cover flap to cover the Spanish on the right.

PIN	**el pin** *el peen*
bank	**el banco** *el bankoh*
cashier	**el cajero** *el kaheroh*
cashpoint/ATM	**el cajero automático** *el kaheroh aootomateekoh*
notes	**los billetes** *los beeyetes*
travellers' cheques	**los cheques de viaje** *los chekes day beeahay*

5 Useful phrases (4 minutes)

Practise these phrases and then test yourself
using the cover flap.

I'd like to change some money.	**Quisiera cambiar dinero.** *keesyairah kambyar deeneroh*
What is the exchange rate?	**¿A cuánto está el cambio?** *ah kwantoh estah el kambyoh*
I'd like to withdraw some money.	**Quisiera sacar dinero.** *keesyairah sakar deeneroh*

6 Say it (2 minutes)

I'd like to change some travellers' cheques.

Do I need my passport?

I'd like a stamp for the United Kingdom.

Meta su pin, por favor.
metah soo peen, por fabor

Please key in your PIN.

¿Tengo que firmar también?
tengoh kay feermar tambyen

Do I have to sign as well?

No, no hace falta.
noh, noh ahthay faltah

No, that's not necessary.

LOS SERVICIOS
Services

You can combine the Spanish words on these pages with the vocabulary you learned in week 10 to help you explain basic problems and cope with arranging most repairs. When organizing construction work or a repair, it's a good idea to agree to the price and method of payment in advance.

1 **Warm up** (1 minute)

What is the Spanish for "doesn't work"? (pp.60-1)

What's the Spanish for "today" and "tomorrow"? (pp.28-9)

2 **Words to remember** (4 minutes)

Familiarize yourself with these words and test yourself using the cover flap.

el fontanero *el fontanairoh*	plumber
el electricista *el ehlektreetheestah*	electrician
el mecánico *el mekaneekoh*	mechanic
el albañil *el albanyeel*	builder
la asistenta *lah aseestentah*	cleaner
el pintor *el peentor*	decorator
el carpintero *el karpeenteroh*	carpenter
el técnico *el tekneekoh*	technician

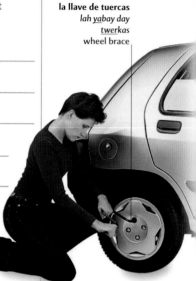

la llave de tuercas
lah yabay day twerkas
wheel brace

No necesito un mecánico.
noh netheseetoh oon mekaneekoh
I don't need a mechanic.

3 **In conversation** (3 minutes)

La lavadora no funciona.
lah labadorah noh foothyonah

The washing machine's not working.

Sí, la manguera está rota.
see, lah mangherah estah rrotah

Yes, the hose is broken.

¿La puede arreglar?
lah pweday arreglar

Can you repair it?

4 Useful phrases (3 minutes)

Practise these phrases and then test yourself using the cover flap.

Can you clean the bathroom?	**¿Puede limpiar el cuarto de baño?** *pweday leempyar el kwartoh day banyoh*
Can you repair the boiler?	**¿Puede arreglar la caldera?** *pweday arreglar lah kalderah*
Do you know a good electrician?	**¿Conoce a un buen electricista?** *konothay ah oon bwen ehlektreetheestah*

¿Dónde me pueden arreglar la plancha?
donday may pweden arreglar lah planchah
Where can I get the iron repaired?

5 Put into practice (4 minutes)

Empiezo el trabajo mañana.
empyaythoh el trabahoh manyanah
I start the job tomorrow.

los planos
los planos
plans

Practise these phrases. Cover the text on the right and complete the dialogue in Spanish. Check your answers and repeat if necessary.

Su verja está rota.
soo berhah estah rrotah

Your gate is broken.

Ask: Do you know a good builder?

¿Conoce a un buen albañil?
konothay ah oon bwen albanyeel

Sí, hay uno en el pueblo.
see, ah-ee oonoh en el pwebloh

Yes, there is one in the village.

Ask: Do you have his phone number?

¿Tiene su número de teléfono?
tyenay soo noomeroh day telefonoh

No, va a necesitar una nueva.
noh, bah ah netheseetar oonah nwebah

No, you'll need a new one.

¿Lo puede hacer hoy?
loh pweday ahther oy

Can you do it today?

No, volveré mañana.
noh, bolberay manyanah

No. I'll come back tomorrow.

1 Warm up (1 minute)

Say the days of the week in Spanish. (pp.28-9)

How do you say "cleaner"? (pp.110-11)

Say "It's 9.30", "10.45", "12.00". (pp.30-1)

VENIR
To come

The verb **venir** (to come) is one of the most useful verbs. As well as the main verb (see below) it is worth knowing the instruction **¡ven!/¡venga!** (come here! informal/formal). Note that with me becomes **conmigo** and with you **contigo**: **ven conmigo** (come with me); **vengo contigo** (I'm going with you).

2 Venir: to come (6 minutes)

Say the different forms of the verb aloud, reading from the table. Use the cover flap to test yourself and, when you are confident, practise the sample sentences below.

Vienen en muchos colores.
beeaynen en moochos kolores
They come in many colours.

yo vengo *yoh bengoh*	I come
tú vienes/usted viene *too byenes/oosted byenay*	you come (informal/formal singular)
él/ella viene *el/eh-yah byenay*	he/she comes
nosotros(-as) venimos *nosotros(-as) beneemos*	we come
vosotros(-as) venís *bosotros(-as) benees*	you come (informal plural)
ustedes vienen *oostedes byenen*	you come (formal plural)
ellos/ellas vienen *eh-yos/eh-yas byenen*	they come

Vengo ahora. *bengoh ah-orah*	I'm coming now.
Venimos todos los martes. *beneemos todos los martes*	We come every Tuesday.
Vienen en tren. *byenen en tren*	They come by train.

Conversational tip To say I come from England in Spanish, you have to use the verb to be, as in **soy inglés** (I am from England). When you use the verb to come, as in **Vengo de Londres**, it means you have just arrived from London.

3 Useful phrases (4 minutes)

Learn these phrases and then test yourself using the cover flap.

When can I come?	**¿Cuándo puedo venir?** _kwandoh pwedoh beneer_
Does it come in size 44?	**¿Viene en la talla 44?** _byenay en lah tayah kwarentah ee kwatroh_
The cleaner comes every Monday.	**La asistenta viene todos los lunes.** _lah aseestentah byenay todos los loones_
Come with me. (informal/formal)	**Ven conmigo/ Venga conmigo.** _ben konmeegoh/ bengah konmeegoh_

¿Puede venir el viernes?
pweday beneer el byairnes
Can you come on Friday?

4 Put into practice (4 minutes)

Practise these phrases. Then cover the text on the right and say the anwering part of the dialogue in Spanish. Check your answers and repeat if necessary.

Peluquería Cristina, dígame.
pelookereeah kristeenah, deegamay

Christine's hair salon. Can I help you?

Say: I'd like an appointment.

Quisiera una cita.
keesyairah oonah theetah

¿Cuándo quiere venir?
kwandoh kyairay beneer

When do you want to come?

Say: Today, if possible.

Hoy, si es posible.
oy, see es poseeblay

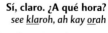

Sí, claro. ¿A qué hora?
see klaroh, ah kay orah

Yes of course. What time?

Say: At 10.30.

A las diez y media.
ah las dyeth ee medeeah

LA POLICÍA Y EL DELITO
Police and crime

1 Warm up (1 minute)

What's the Spanish for "big" and "small"? (pp.64-5)

Say "The room is big" and "The bed is small". (pp.64-5)

While in Spain, if you are the victim of a crime, you should go to the police station to report it, or in an emergency, you can dial 112. You may have to explain your complaint in Spanish, so some basic vocabulary is useful.

2 Words to remember: crime (4 minutes)

Familiarize yourself with these words.

Necesito un abogado.
netheseetoh oon abogadoh
I need a lawyer.

el robo _el rroboh_	robbery
la denuncia _lah denoontheeah_	police report
el ladrón _el ladron_	thief
la policía _lah poleetheeah_	police
la declaración _lah deklarathyon_	statement
el testigo _el testeegoh_	witness
el abogado _el abogadoh_	lawyer

3 Useful phrases (3 minutes)

Learn these phrases and then test yourself.

Me han robado. _may an rrobadoh_	I've been robbed.
¿Qué han robado? _kay an rrobadoh_	What was stolen?
¿Vió quién lo hizo? _byoh kyain loh eethoh_	Did you see who did it?
¿Cuándo ocurrió? _kwandoh okoorryoh_	When did it happen?

la cámara de fotos
lah kamarah day fotos
camera

la cartera
la karterah
purse

4 Words to remember: appearance (5 minutes)

Learn these words. Remember some adjectives have a feminine form.

man	**el hombre** *el ombray*
woman	**la mujer** *lah moo-hair*
tall	**alto/alta** *altoh/altah*
short	**bajo/baja** *bahoh/bahah*
young	**joven** *hoben*
old	**viejo/vieja** *byayhoh/byayhah*
fat	**gordo/gorda** *gordoh/gordah*
thin	**delgado/delgada** *delgadoh/delgadah*
long/short hair	**el pelo largo/corto** *el peloh largoh/kortoh*
glasses	**las gafas** *las gafas*
beard	**la barba** *la barbah*

Él es bajo y tiene bigote.
el es bahoh ee tyenay beegotay
He is short and has a moustache.

Tiene el pelo negro y corto.
tyenay el peloh negroh ee kortoh
He has short, black hair.

Cultural tip In Spain there is a difference between **la guardia civil** and **la policía**. **La policía** are the local police while **la guardia civil** operates in airports and patrols the national road system. The police uniforms are blue and those of the **guardia civil** are green.

5 Put into practice (2 minutes)

Practise these phrases. Then cover the text on the right and follow the instructions to make your reply in Spanish.

¿Cómo era?
komoh ehrah

What did he look like?

Say: Short and fat.

Bajo y gordo.
bahoh ee gordoh

¿Y el pelo?
ee el peloh

And his hair?

Say: Long with a beard.

Largo y con barba.
largoh ee kon barbah

REPASE Y REPITA
Review and repeat

1 To come

❶ vienen
byenen

❷ viene
byenay

❸ venimos
beneemos

❹ venís
benees

❺ vengo
bengoh

1 To come (3 minutes)

Put the correct form of **venir** (*to come*) in the gaps.

❶ Mis padres _____ a las cuatro.

❷ La asistenta _____ una vez a la semana.

❸ Nosotros _____ todos los martes.

❹ ¿ _____ vosotros con nosotros?

❺ Yo _____ en taxi.

2 Bank and post

❶ los billetes
los beeyetes

❷ la postal
lah postal

❸ el paquete
el paketay

❹ el sobre
el sobray

2 Bank and post (4 minutes)

Name these items.

❶ notes

postcard ❷

❸ parcel

envelope ❹

3 Appearance (4 minutes)

What do these descriptions mean?

❶ Es un hombre alto y delgado.

❷ Ella tiene el pelo corto y gafas.

❸ Soy baja y tengo el pelo largo.

❹ Ella es vieja y gorda.

❺ Él tiene los ojos azules y barba.

3 Appearance

❶ He's a tall, thin man.

❷ She has short hair and glasses.

❸ I'm short and I have long hair.

❹ She's old and fat.

❺ He has blue eyes and a beard.

4 The pharmacy (4 minutes)

You are asking a pharmacist for advice. Join in the conversation, replying in Spanish following the English prompts.

    Buenos días, ¿qué desea?
❶ I have a cough.

    ¿Le duele el pecho?
❷ No, but I have a headache.

    Tiene estas pastillas.
❸ Do you have that as a syrup?

    Sí señor. Aquí tiene.
❹ Thank you. How much is that?

    Cuatro euros.
❺ Here you are. Goodbye.

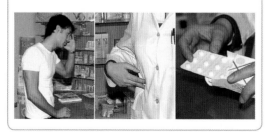

4 The pharmacy

❶ Tengo tos.
tengoh tos

❷ No, pero me duele la cabeza.
noh, peroh may dwelay lah kabethah

❸ ¿Lo tiene en jarabe?
loh tyenay en harabay

❹ Gracias. ¿Cuánto es?
grathyas. kwantoh es

❺ Aquí tiene. Adiós.
ahkee tyenay. addy-os

1 Warm up (1 minute)

What is the Spanish for "museum" and "art gallery"? (pp.48-9)

Say "I don't like the curtains". (pp.100-1)

Ask "Do you want...?" informally. (pp.22-3)

EL OCIO
Leisure time

The Spanish pride themselves on their lively nightlife and love for the arts, including theatre and film. It is not unusual for Spaniards to number politics or philosophy among their interests. Be prepared for these topics to be the subject of conversation in social situations.

2 Words to remember (4 minutes)

Familiarize yourself with these words and test yourself using the cover flap to conceal the Spanish on the left.

el teatro el te-_ahtroh_	theatre
el cine el _theenay_	cinema
la discoteca lah deesko_tekah_	discotheque
el deporte el de_portay_	sport
el turismo el too_reesmoh_	sightseeing
la política la po_leeteekah_	politics
la música lah moo_seekah_	music
el arte el _artay_	art

Me encanta el baile.
me en_kan_tah el _baeelay_
I love dancing.

3 In conversation (4 minutes)

Hola. ¿Quieres jugar al tenis hoy?
o-lah. _kyaires_ hoo_gar_ al _tenis_ oy

Hi, do you want to play tennis today?

No, no me gusta el deporte.
noh, noh may _goostah_ el de_portay_

No, I don't like sport.

Y entonces, ¿qué te gusta?
ee en_ton_thes, kay tay _goostah_

So then, what do you like?

los video-juegos
los beedayoh-hwegos
video games

la bailadora
lah baeeladorah
dancer

el traje típico
el trahay teepeekoh
traditional costume

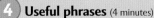

4 Useful phrases (4 minutes)

Learn these phrases and then test yourself using the cover flap.

What are your (formal/informal) interests?	**¿Cuáles son sus/tus intereses?** *kwales son soos/toos intereses*
I like the theatre.	**Me gusta el teatro.** *may goostah el te-ahtroh*
I prefer the cinema.	**Yo prefiero el cine.** *yoh prefyairoh el theenay*
I'm interested in art.	**Me interesa el arte.** *may interesah el artay*
That bores me.	**Eso me aburre.** *ehsoh may aboorray*

5 Say it (2 minutes)

I'm interested in music.

I prefer sport.

I don't like video games.

Prefiero el turismo e ir de compras.
prefyairoh el tooreesmoh eh eer day kompras

I prefer sightseeing and shopping.

Eso a mí no me interesa.
ehsoh ah mee noh may interesah

That doesn't interest me.

No pasa nada. Me voy yo sola.
noh pasah nadah. may boy yoh solah

No problem. I'll go on my own.

EL DEPORTE Y LOS PASATIEMPOS
Sport and hobbies

1 **Warm up** (1 minute)

Ask "Do you (formal) want to play tennis?" (pp.118-19)

Say "I like the theatre" and "I prefer sightseeing". (pp.118-19)

Say "That doesn't interest me". (pp.118-19)

Hacer (*to do* or *to make*) and **jugar** (*to play*) are the verbs used most when talking about sport and pastimes. **Jugar** is followed by **al** when you are talking about playing a sport, as in **juego al baloncesto** (*I play basketball*).

2 **Words to remember** (5 minutes)

Familiarize yourself with these words and then test yourself.

el fútbol/rugby *el footbol/roogbee*	football/rugby
el tenis/baloncesto *el tenis/balonthestoh*	tennis/basketball
la natación *lah natathyon*	swimming
la vela *lah belah*	sailing
la pesca *lah peskah*	fishing
la pintura *lah peentoorah*	painting
el ciclismo *el theekleesmoh*	cycling
el senderismo *el sendereesmoh*	hiking

el búnker
el bunker
bunker

el jugador de golf
el hugador day golf
golfer

Juego al golf todos los días.
hwegoh al golf todos los deeyas
I play golf every day.

3 **Useful phrases** (2 minutes)

Learn these phrases and then test yourself.

Juego al fútbol. *hwegoh al footbol*	I play football.
Juega al tenis. *hwegah al tenis*	He plays tennis.
Ella pinta. *eh-yah peentah*	She paints.

4 Hacer: to do or to make (4 minutes)

Hoy hace bueno.
oy ahthay bwenoh
It's nice (weather) today.

___ **la banderola**
lah bandairolah
flag

___ **el campo de golf**
el kampoh day golf
golf course

Hacer is a useful verb meaning *to do* or *to make*.
It is commonly used to describe leisure pursuits.
Hace is also used to describe the weather.

I do	**yo hago** *yoh ahgoh*
you do (informal/ formal singular)	**tú haces/usted hace** *too ahthes/oosted ahthay*
he/she does	**él/ella hace** *el/eh-yah ahthay*
we do	**nosotros(-as) hacemos** *nosotros(-as) ahthemos*
you do (informal plural)	**vosotros(-as) hacéis** *bosotros(-as) ahthays*
you do (formal plural)	**ustedes hacen** *oostedes ahthen*
they do	**ellos/ellas hacen** *eh-yos/eh-yas ahthen*
What do you like doing? (informal/formal singular)	**¿Qué te/le gusta hacer?** *kay tay/lay goostah ahthair?*
I go hiking.	**Yo hago senderismo.** *yoh ahgoh sendereesmoh*

5 Put into practice (3 minutes)

Join in this conversation following the English prompts.

¿Qué te gusta hacer?
kay tay goostah ahthair
What do you like doing?

Say: I like playing tennis.

Me gusta jugar al tenis.
may goostah hoogar al tenis

¿Juegas al fútbol también?
hwegas al footbol tambyen
Do you play football as well?

Say: No, I play rugby.

No, juego al rugby.
noh, hwegoh al roogbee

¿Cuándo juegas?
kwandoh hwegas
When do you play?

Say: I play every week.

Juego todas las semanas.
hwegoh todas las semanas

LA VIDA SOCIAL
Socializing

Say "my husband" and "my wife". (pp.10-11)

Say the days of the week in Spanish. (pp.28-9)

Say "Sorry, I'm busy". (pp.32-3)

The dinner table is the centre of the Spanish social world. You can expect to do a lot of your socializing around the table, enjoying food and wine. In general it is best to use the more polite **usted** form to talk to older people and **tú** with the younger crowd.

2 **Useful phrases** (3 minutes)

la invitada
lah inbeetadah
guest

Practise these phrases and then test yourself.

Me gustaría invitarte a cenar. *may goostareeah inbeetartay ah thenar*	I'd like to invite you to dinner.
¿Estás libre el miércoles que viene? *estas leebray el myairkoles kay byenay*	Are you free next Wednesday?
Quizá otro día. *keethah ohtroh deeyah*	Perhaps another day.

Cultural tip When you visit someone's house for the first time, it is usual to bring flowers or wine. If you are invited again, having seen your host's house, you can bring something a little more personal.

3 **In conversation** (3 minutes)

¿Quieres venir a comer el martes?
kyaires beneer ah komer el martes

Would you like to come to lunch on Tuesday?

Lo siento, estoy ocupada.
loh syaintoh, estoy okoopadah

I'm sorry, I'm busy.

¿Qué tal el jueves?
kay tal el hwebes

What about Thursday?

la anfitriona
lah anfeetryonah
hostess

4 **Words to remember** (3 minutes)

Familiarize yourself with these words and test yourself using the flap.

party	**la fiesta** *lah fyaystah*
dinner party	**la cena** *lah thenah*
invitation	**la invitación** *lah inbeetathyon*
reception	**la recepción** *lah rrethepthyon*
cocktail party	**el coctel** *el koktel*

5 **Put into practice** (5 minutes)

Join this conversation, replying in Spanish.

¿Puede venir a una recepción esta noche?
pweday beneer ah oonah rrethepthyon estah nochay

Can you come to a reception tonight?

Say: Yes, I'd love to.

Sí, encantado/-a.
see, enkan-tadoh/-ah

Empieza a las ocho.
empyaythah ah las ochoh

It starts at eight o'clock.

Ask: What should I wear?

¿Qué me pongo?
kay may pongoh

Gracias por invitarnos.
grathyas por inbeetarnos
Thank you for inviting us.

Encantada.
enkan-tadah

I'd be delighted.

Ven con tu marido.
ben kon too mareedoh

Bring your husband.

Gracias, ¿a qué hora?
grathyas, ah kay orah

Thank you, at what time?

Respuestas
Answers (Cover with flap)

REPASE Y REPITA
Review and repeat

1 Animals

❶ **el pez**
el peth

❷ **el pájaro**
el paharoh

❸ **el conejo**
el konehoh

❹ **el gato**
el gatoh

❺ **el hámster**
el hamster

❻ **el perro**
el perroh

1 Animals (3 minutes)

Name the numbered animals in Spanish.

rabbit ❸

❶ fish

hamster ❺

❹ cat

2 I like...

❶ **Me gusta el fútbol.**
may goostah el footbol

❷ **No me gusta el golf.**
noh may goostah el golf

❸ **Me gusta pintar.**
may goostah peentar

❹ **No me gustan las flores.**
noh may goostan las flores

2 I like ... (4 minutes)

Say the following in Spanish:

❶ I like football.
❷ I don't like golf.
❸ I like painting.
❹ I don't like flowers.

2 bird

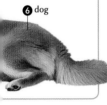

6 dog

3 Hacer (4 minutes)

Use the correct form of the verb **hacer** (*to do* or *to make*) in these sentences.

1 Vosotros _____ senderismo.

2 Ella _____ eso todos los días.

3 ¿Qué _____ tú?

4 Hoy no _____ frío.

5 ¿Qué _____ ellos esta noche?

6 Yo _____ natación.

3 Hacer

1 hacéis
ah*thays*

2 hace
ah*thay*

3 haces
ah*thes*

4 hace
ah*thay*

5 hacen
ah*then*

6 hago
*ah*goh

4 An invitation (4 minutes)

You are invited for dinner. Join in the conversation, replying in Spanish following the English prompts.

¿Quieres venir a comer el viernes?
1 I'm sorry, I'm busy.

¿Qué tal el sábado?
2 I'd be delighted.

Ven con los niños.
3 Thank you. What time?

A las doce y media.
4 That's good for me.

4 An invitation

1 Lo siento, estoy ocupado/-a.
loh *syen*toh, es*toy* okoo*pa*doh/-ah

2 Encantado/-a.
enkan*ta*doh/-ah

3 Gracias. ¿A qué hora?
*grathyas. ah kay *o*rah

4 Me viene bien.
may *byen*ay byen

Reinforce and progress

Regular practice is the key to maintaining and advancing your language skills. In this section you will find a variety of suggestions for reinforcing and extending your knowledge of Spanish. Many involve returning to exercises in the book and using the dictionaries to extend their scope. Go back through the lessons in a different order, mix and match activities to make up your own 15-minute daily programme, or focus on topics that are of particular relevance to your current needs.

1 Warm up (1 minute)

Say "he is" and "they are". (pp.14–15)

Say "he is not" and "they are not". (pp.14–15)

What is Spanish for "the children"? (pp.10–11)

3 I'd like... (3 minutes)

Say "I'd like" the following:

❶ black coffee   churros ❷   ❸ sugar

white coffee ❹

Keep warmed up
Re-visit the Warm Up boxes to remind yourself of key words and phrases. Make sure you work your way through all of them on a regular basis.

Review and repeat again
Work through a Review and Repeat lesson as a way of reinforcing words and phrases presented in the course. Return to the main lesson for any topic on which you are no longer confident.

3 In conversation: taxi (2 minutes)

Carry on conversing
Re-read the In Conversation panels. Say both parts of the conversation, paying attention to the pronunciation. Where possible, try incorporating new words from the dictionary.

A la Plaza de España, por favor.
ah lah plathah day espanyah, por fabor

Plaza de España, please.

Sí, de acuerdo, señor.
see, day akwairdo, senyor

Yes, certainly, sir.

¿Me puede dejar aquí, por favor?
may pweday dehar ahkee, por fabor

Can you drop me here, please?

3 Useful phrases (5 minutes)

Practise these phrases and then test yourself using the cover flap.

| The room is too cold/hot. | **Hace demasiado frío/calor en la habitación.** *ahthay daymasyahdoh freeoh/kalor en lah abeetathyon* |

| There are no towels. | **No hay toallas.** *noh ah-ee toh-ahyas* |

| I need some soap. | **Necesito jabón.** *netheseetoh habon* |

Practise phrases
Return to the Useful Phrases and Put into Practice exercises. Test yourself using the cover flap. When you are confident, devise your own versions of the phrases, using new words from the dictionary.

| The shower doesn't work. | **La ducha no funciona.** *lah doochah noh foonthyonah* |

Match, repeat, and extend
Remind yourself of words related to specific topics by returning to the Match and Repeat and Words to Remember exercises. Test yourself using the cover flap. Discover new words in that area by referring to the dictionary and menu guide.

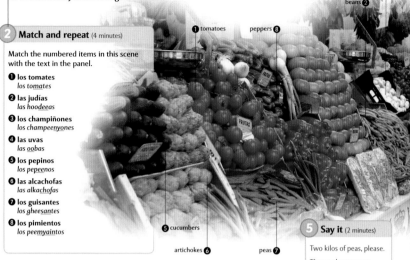

mushrooms ❸
beans ❷
❶ tomatoes   peppers ❽

2 Match and repeat (4 minutes)

Match the numbered items in this scene with the text in the panel.

❶ **los tomates**
   los to*mates*

❷ **las judías**
   las hoo*dee*as

❸ **los champiñones**
   los champeeny*ones*

❹ **las uvas**
   las *oo*bas

❺ **los pepinos**
   los pe*pee*nos

❻ **las alcachofas**
   las alka*cho*fas

❼ **los guisantes**
   los ghee*sant*es

❽ **los pimientos**
   los peemy*ain*tos

❺ cucumbers

artichokes ❻   peas ❼

Say it again
The Say It exercises are a useful instant reminder for each lesson. Practise these, using your own vocabulary variations from the dictionary or elsewhere in the lesson.

5 Say it (2 minutes)

Two kilos of peas, please.

The mushrooms are too expensive.

How much are the grapes?

Using other resources

In addition to working with this book, try the following language extension ideas:

Visit a Spanish-speaking country and try out your new skills with native speakers. Find out if there is a Spanish community near you. There may be shops, cafés, restaurants, and clubs. Try to visit some of these and use your Spanish to order food and drink and strike up conversations. Most native speakers will be happy to speak Spanish to you.

Join a language class or club. There are usually evening and day classes available at different levels. Or you could start a club yourself if you have friends who are also interested in keeping up their Spanish.

Look at Spanish magazines and newspapers. The pictures will help you to understand the text. Advertisements are also a useful way of expanding your vocabulary.

Use the Internet, where you can find all kinds of websites for learning languages, some of which offer free online help and activities. You can also find Spanish websites for everything from renting a house to shampooing your pet. You can even access Spanish radio and TV stations online. Start by going to a Spanish search engine, such as ozu.es, and keying in a hobby or sport that interests you, or set yourself a challenge, such as finding a two-bedroom house for rent in Madrid.

MENU GUIDE

This guide lists the most common terms you may encounter on Spanish menus or when shopping for food. If you can't find an exact phrase, try looking up its component parts.

A

aceitunas *olives*
acelgas *spinach beet*
achicoria *chicory*
aguacate *avocado*
ahumados *smoked*
agua mineral *mineral water*
ajo *garlic*
al ajillo *with garlic*
a la parrilla *grilled*
a la plancha *grilled*
albaricoques *apricots*
albóndigas *meatballs*
alcachofas *artichokes*
alcaparras *capers*
al horno *baked*
allioli *garlic mayonnaise*
almejas *clams*
almejas a la marinera *clams stewed in wine and parsley*
almejas naturales *live clams*
almendras *almonds*
almíbar *syrup*
alubias *beans*
ancas de rana *frogs' legs*
anchoas *anchovies*
anguila *eel*
angulas *baby eels*
arenque *herring*
arroz a la cubana *rice with fried eggs and banana fritters*
arroz a la valenciana *rice with seafood*
arroz con leche *rice pudding*
asados *roast meat*
atún *tuna*
azúcar *sugar*

B

bacalao a la vizcaína *cod served with ham, peppers, and chillies*
bacalao al pil pil *cod served with chillies and garlic*
batido *milk shake*
bebidas *drinks*
berenjenas *aubergine*
besugo al horno *baked sea bream*
bistec de ternera *veal steak*
bonito *fish similar to tuna*
boquerones fritos *fried, fresh anchovies*
brazo gitano *swiss roll*
brocheta de riñones *kidney kebabs*
buñuelos *fried pastries*
butifarra *Catalan sausage*

C

cabrito asado *roast kid*
cacahuetes *peanuts*
cachelada *pork stew with eggs, tomato, and onion*
café *coffee*
café con leche *coffee with steamed milk*
calabacines *courgette*
calabaza *pumpkin*
calamares a la romana *squid rings in batter*
calamares en su tinta *squid cooked in their ink*
caldeirada *fish soup*
caldereta gallega *vegetable stew*
caldo de ... ... *soup*
caldo de gallina *chicken soup*
caldo de pescado *clear fish soup*
caldo gallego *vegetable soup*
caldo guanche *soup of potatoes, tomatoes, onions, and courgettes*
callos a la madrileña *tripe cooked with chillies*
camarones *baby prawns*
canela *cinnamon*
cangrejos *crabs*
caracoles *snails*
caramelos *sweets*
carnes *meats*
castañas *chestnuts*
cebolla *onion*
cebolletas *spring onions*
centollo *spider crab*
cerdo *pork*
cerezas *cherries*
cerveza *beer*
cesta de frutas *selection of fresh fruit*
champiñones *mushrooms*
chanquetes *fish (similar to whitebait)*
chipirones *baby squid*
chipirones en su tinta *squid cooked in their ink*
chocos *cuttlefish*
chorizo *spicy sausage*
chuleta de buey *beef chop*
chuleta de cerdo *pork chop*
chuleta de cerdo empanada *breaded pork chop*
chuleta de cordero *lamb chop*
chuleta de cordero empanada *breaded lamb chop*
chuleta de ternera *veal chop*
chuleta de ternera empanada *breaded veal chop*
chuletas de lomo ahumado *smoked pork chops*
chuletitas de cordero *small lamb chops*
chuletón *large chop*
chuletón de buey *large beef chop*
churros *deep-fried pastry strips*
cigalas *crayfish*
cigalas cocidas *boiled crayfish*
ciruelas *plums*
ciruelas pasas *prunes*
cochinillo asado *roast suckling pig*
cocido *meat, chickpea, and vegetable stew*
cocktail de bogavante *lobster cocktail*
cocochas (de merluza) *hake stew*
cóctel de gambas *prawn cocktail*
cóctel de langostinos *jumbo prawn cocktail*
cóctel de mariscos *seafood cocktail*
codornices *quail*
codornices escabechadas *marinated quail*
codornices estofadas *braised quail*
col *cabbage*
coles de Bruselas *Brussels sprouts*
coliflor *cauliflower*
coñac *brandy*
conejo *rabbit*

conejo encebollado *rabbit with onions*
congrio *conger eel*
consomé con yema *consommé with egg yolk*
consomé de ave *fowl consommé*
contra de ternera con guisantes *veal stew with peas*
contrafilete de ternera *veal fillet*
copa *glass (of wine)*
copa de helado *ice cream, assorted flavours*
cordero asado *roast lamb*
cordero chilindrón *lamb stew with onion, tomato, peppers, and eggs*
costillas de cerdo *pork ribs*
crema catalana *crème brûlée*
cremada *dessert made with egg, sugar, and milk*
crema de... *cream of ... soup*
crema de legumbres *cream of vegetable soup*
crepe imperiale *crêpe suzette*
criadillas de tierra *truffles*
crocante *ice cream with chopped nuts*
croquetas *croquettes*
cuajada *curds*

D, E

dátiles *dates*
embutidos *sausages*
embutidos de la tierra *local sausages*
empanada gallega *fish pie*
empanada santiaguesa *fish pie*
empanadillas *small pies*
endivia *endive*
en escabeche *marinated*
ensalada *salad*
ensalada de arenque *fish salad*
ensalada ilustrada *mixed salad*
ensalada mixta *mixed salad*
ensalada simple *green salad*
ensaladilla rusa *Russian salad (potatoes, carrots, peas, and other vegetables in mayonnaise)*
entrecot a la parrilla *grilled entrecôte*
entremeses *hors d'oeuvres, starters*
escalope a la milanesa *breaded veal with cheese*
escalope a la parrilla *grilled veal*
escalope a la plancha *grilled veal*
escalope de lomo de cerdo *escalope of pork fillet*
escalope de ternera *veal escalope*

escalope empanado *breaded escalope*
escalopines al vino de Marsala *veal escalopes cooked in Marsala wine*
escalopines de ternera *veal escalopes*
espadín a la toledana *kebab*
espaguetis *spaghetti*
espárragos *asparagus*
espárragos trigueros *wild green asparagus*
espinacas *spinach*
espinazo de cerdo con patatas *stew of pork ribs with potatoes*
estofado *braised; stew*
estragón *tarragon*

F

fabada (asturiana) *bean stew with sausage*
faisán *pheasant*
faisán trufado *pheasant with truffles*
fiambres *cold meats*
fideos *thin pasta, noodles*
filete a la parrilla *grilled beef steak*
filete de cerdo *pork steak*
filete de ternera *veal steak*
flan *crème caramel*
frambuesas *raspberries*
fresas *strawberries*
fritos *fried*
fruta *fruit*

G

gallina en pepitoria *chicken stew with peppers*
gambas *prawns*
gambas cocidas *boiled prawns*
gambas en gabardina *prawns in batter*
gambas rebozadas *prawns in batter*
garbanzos *chickpeas*
garbanzos a la catalana *chickpeas with sausage, boiled eggs, and pine nuts*
gazpacho andaluz *cold tomato soup*
gelatina de ... ... *jelly*
gratén de ... ... *au gratin (baked in a cream and cheese sauce)*
granizada *crushed ice drink*
gratinada/o *au gratin*
grelo *turnip*
grillado *grilled*
guisantes *peas*
guisantes salteados *sautéed peas*

H

habas *broad beans*
habichuelas *white beans*
helado *ice cream*
helado de vainilla *vanilla ice cream*
helado de turrón *nougat ice cream*
hígado *liver*
hígado de ternera *calves' liver*
hígado estofado *braised liver*
higos con miel y nueces *figs with honey and nuts*
higos secos *dried figs*
horchata (de chufas) *cold drink made from chufa nuts*
huevo hilado *egg yolk garnish*
huevos *eggs*
huevos a la flamenca *fried eggs with ham, tomato, and vegetables*
huevos cocidos *hard-boiled eggs*
huevos con patatas fritas *fried eggs and chips*
huevos con picadillo *eggs with minced meat*
huevos duros *hard-boiled eggs*
huevos escalfados *poached eggs*
huevos pasados por agua *soft-boiled eggs*
huevos revueltos *scrambled eggs*

J

jamón *ham*
jamón con huevo hilado *ham with egg yolk garnish*
jamón serrano *cured ham*
jarra de vino *wine jug*
jerez *sherry*
jeta *pigs' cheeks*
judías verdes *green beans*
judías verdes a la española *bean stew*
judías verdes al natural *plain green beans*
jugo de ... ... *juice*

L

langosta *lobster*
langosta a la americana *lobster with brandy and garlic*
langosta a la catalana *lobster with mushrooms and ham in white sauce*
langosta fría con mayonesa *cold lobster with mayonnaise*
langostinos *king prawns*
langostinos dos salsas *king prawns cooked in two sauces*
laurel *bay leaves*

leche *milk*
leche frita *pudding made from milk and eggs*
leche merengada *cold milk with meringue*
lechuga *lettuce*
lengua de buey *ox tongue*
lengua de cordero *lambs' tongue*
lenguado a la romana *sole in batter*
lenguado meuniere *sole meunière (floured sole fried in butter)*
lentejas *lentils*
lentejas aliñadas *lentils in vinaigrette dressing*
licores *spirits, liqueurs*
liebre estofada *stewed hare*
lima *lime*
limón *lemon*
lombarda *red cabbage*
lomo curado *pork loin sausage*
lonchas de jamón *sliced, cured ham*
longaniza *cooked Spanish sausage*
lubina *sea bass*
lubina a la marinera *sea bass in a parsley sauce*

M

macedonia de fruta *fruit salad*
mahonesa or mayonesa *mayonnaise*
Málaga *a sweet wine*
mandarinas *tangerines*
manitas de cordero *lamb shank*
manos de cerdo *pigs' feet*
manos de cerdo a la parrilla *grilled pigs' feet*
mantecadas *small sponge cakes*
mantequilla *butter*
manzanas *apples*
mariscada *cold mixed shellfish*
mariscos del día *fresh shellfish*
mariscos del tiempo *seasonal shellfish*
medallones *steaks*
media de agua *half bottle of mineral water*
mejillones *mussels*
mejillones a la marinera *mussels in a wine sauce*
melocotón *peach*
melón *melon*
menestra de legumbres *vegetable stew*
menú de la casa *set menu*
menú del día *set menu*
merluza *hake*
merluza a la cazuela *stewed hake*

merluza al ajo arriero *hake with garlic and chillies*
merluza a la riojana *hake with chillies*
merluza a la romana *hake steaks in batter*
merluza a la vasca *hake in a garlic sauce*
merluza en salsa *hake in sauce*
merluza en salsa verde *hake in a green (parsley and wine) sauce*
merluza fría *cold hake*
merluza frita *fried hake*
mermelada *jam*
mero *grouper (fish)*
mero en salsa verde *grouper in green (garlic and parsley) sauce*
mollejas de ternera fritas *fried sweetbreads*
morcilla *blood sausage*
morcilla de carnero *mutton blood sausage*
morros de cerdo *pigs' cheeks*
morros de vaca *cows' cheeks*
mortadela *salami-type sausage*
morteruelo *kind of pâté*

N, O

nabo *turnip*
naranjas *oranges*
nata *cream*
natillas *cold custard*
níscalos *wild mushrooms*
nueces *walnuts*
orejas de cerdo *pigs' ears*

P

paella *fried rice with seafood and/or meat*
paella castellana *meat paella*
paella valenciana *shellfish, rabbit, and chicken paella*
paleta de cordero lechal *shoulder of lamb*
pan *bread*
panache de verduras *vegetable stew*
panceta *bacon*
parrillada de caza *mixed grilled game*
parrillada de mariscos *mixed grilled shellfish*
pasas *raisins*
pastel de ternera *veal pie*
pasteles *cakes*
patatas a la pescadora *potatoes with fish*
patatas asadas *baked potatoes*
patatas bravas *potatoes in spicy tomato sauce*
patatas fritas *chips*

patitos rellenos *stuffed duckling*
pato a la naranja *duck in orange sauce*
pavo *turkey*
pavo trufado *turkey stuffed with truffles*
pecho de ternera *breast of veal*
pechuga de pollo *breast of chicken*
pepinillos *gherkins*
pepino *cucumber*
peras *pears*
percebes *edible barnacle*
perdices a la campesina *partridges with vegetables*
perdices a la manchega *partridges in red wine, garlic, herbs, and pepper*
perdices escabechadas *marinated partridges*
perejil *parsley*
perritos calientes *hot dogs*
pescaditos fritos *fried fish*
pestiños *sugared pastries flavoured with aniseed*
pez espada *swordfish*
picadillo de ternera *minced veal*
pimienta *black pepper*
pimientos *peppers*
pimientos a la riojana *baked red peppers fried in oil and garlic*
pimientos morrones *a type of bell pepper*
pimientos verdes *green peppers*
piña al gratín *pineapple au gratin*
piña fresca *fresh pineapple*
pinchitos/pinchos *kebabs, snacks served in bars*
pinchos morunos *pork kebabs*
piñones *pine nuts*
pisto *ratatouille*
pisto manchego *vegetable marrow with onion and tomato*
plátanos *bananas*
plátanos flameados *flambéed bananas*
pollo *chicken*
pollo a la riojana *chicken with peppers and chillies*
pollo al ajillo *fried chicken with garlic*
pollo asado *roast chicken*
pollo braseado *braised chicken*
pollo en cacerola *chicken casserole*
pollo en pepitoria *chicken in wine with saffron, garlic, and almonds*
pollos tomateros con zanahorias *young chicken with carrots*
pomelo *grapefruit*
potaje castellano *thick broth*
potaje de ... ... *stew*

puchero canario *casserole of meat, chickpeas, and corn*
pulpitos con cebolla *baby octopus with onions*
pulpo *octopus*
puré de patatas *mashed potatoes, potato purée*
purrusalda *cod with leeks and potatoes*

Q

queso con membrillo *cheese with quince jelly*
queso de bola *Dutch cheese*
queso de Burgos *soft white cheese*
queso del país *local cheese*
queso de oveja *sheep's cheese*
queso gallego *a creamy cheese*
queso manchego *a hard, strong cheese*
quisquillas *shrimps*

R

rábanos *radishes*
ragout de ternera *veal ragoût*
rape a la americana *monkfish with brandy and herbs*
rape a la cazuela *stewed monkfish*
raya *skate*
rebozado *in batter*
redondo al horno *roast fillet of beef*
rellenos *stuffed*
remolacha *beetroot*
repollo *cabbage*
repostería de la casa *cakes baked on the premises*
requesón *cream cheese, cottage cheese*
revuelto de ... *scrambled eggs with ...*
revuelto de ajos tiernos *scrambled eggs with spring garlic*
revuelto de trigueros *scrambled eggs with asparagus*
revuelto mixto *scrambled eggs with mixed vegetables*
riñones *kidneys*
rodaballo *turbot (fish)*
romero *rosemary*
ron *rum*
roscas *sweet pastries*

S

sal *salt*
salchichas *sausages*
salchichas de Frankfurt *hot dog sausages*
salchichón *sausage similar to salami*
salmón ahumado *smoked salmon*
salmonetes *red mullet*
salmonetes en papillote *red mullet cooked in foil*
salmón frío *cold salmon*
salmorejo *sauce of bread, tomatoes, oil, vinegar, green pepper, and garlic*
salpicón de mariscos *shellfish in vinaigrette*
salsa bechamel *white sauce*
salsa holandesa *hollandaise sauce*
sandía *watermelon*
sardinas a la brasa *barbecued sardines*
seco *dry*
semidulce *medium-sweet*
sesos *brains*
sesos a la romana *fried brains in batter*
sesos rebozados *brains in batter*
setas *mushrooms*
sidra *cider*
sobreasada *sausage with cayenne pepper*
solomillo *fillet steak*
solomillo con patatas *fillet steak with chips*
solomillo de ternera *fillet of veal*
solomillo de vaca *fillet of beef*
solomillo frío *cold roast beef*
sopa *soup*
sopa castellana *vegetable soup*
sopa de almendras *almond soup*
sopa de cola de buey *oxtail soup*
sopa de gallina *chicken soup*
sopa del día *soup of the day*
sopa de legumbres *vegetable soup*
sopa de marisco *fish and shellfish soup*
sopa de rabo de buey *oxtail soup*
sopa mallorquina *soup of tomato, meat, and eggs*
sopa sevillana *fish and mayonnaise soup*
soufflé de fresones *strawberry soufflé*

T

tallarines *noodles*
tallarines a la italiana *tagliatelle*
tarta *cake*
tarta de la casa *cake baked on the premises*
tarta de manzana *apple tart*
tencas *tench*
ternera asada *roast veal*
tocinillos del cielo *a very sweet crème caramel*
tomates *tomatoes*
tomillo *thyme*
torrijas *sweet pastries*
tortilla a la paisana *vegetable omelette*
tortilla a su gusto *omelette made to the customer's wishes*
tortilla de escabeche *fish omelette*
tortilla española *Spanish omelette with potato, onion, and garlic*
tortilla sacromonte *vegetable, brains, and sausage omelette*
tortillas variadas *assorted omelettes*
tournedó *fillet steak*
trucha *trout*
trucha ahumada *smoked trout*
trucha escabechada *marinated trout*
truchas a la marinera *trout in wine sauce*
truchas molinera *trout meunière (floured trout fried in butter)*
trufas *truffles*
turrón *nougat*

U, V

uvas *grapes*
verduras *vegetables*
vieiras *scallops*
vino de mesa/blanco / rosado/tinto *table/ white/rosé/ red wine*

Z

zanahorias a la crema *creamed carrots*
zarzuela de mariscos *seafood stew*
zarzuela de pescados y mariscos *fish and shellfish stew*
zumo de ... ... *juice*

DICTIONARY
English to Spanish

The gender of a Spanish noun is indicated by the word for *the*: **el** and
la (masculine and feminine singular) or their plural forms **los** (masculine)
and **las** (feminine). Spanish adjectives (adj) vary according to the gender
and number of the word they describe, and the masculine form is shown
here. In general, adjectives that end in **-o** adopt an **-a** ending in the
feminine form, and those that end in **-e** usually stay the same. For
the plural form, an **-s** is added.

A

a **un/una**
able: to be able **poder**
about: about sixteen
 alrededor de dieciséis
accelerator **el acelerador**
accident **el accidente**
accommodation
 el alojamiento
accountant **el/la contable**
ache **el dolor**
adaptor **el adaptador**
address **la dirección**
adhesive **el pegamento**
admission charge **el precio**
 de entrada
after ... **después de ...**
aftershave **el after-shave**
again **otra vez**
against **contra**
agenda **el orden del día**
agency **la agencia**
AIDS **el Sida**
air **el aire**
air conditioning **el aire**
 acondicionado
aircraft **el avión**
airline **la compañía aérea**
air mail **por avión**
air mattress **la colchoneta**
airport **el aeropuerto**
airport bus **el autobús**
 del aeropuerto
aisle **el pasillo**
alarm clock **el despertador**
alcohol **el alcohol**
Algeria **Argelia**
all **todo;** *all the streets*
 todas las calles;
 that's all **eso es todo**
allergic **alérgico**
almost **casi**
alone **solo**
already **ya**
always **siempre**
am: I am **soy/estoy**

ambulance **la ambulancia**
America **América**
American **el americano/**
 la americana
and **y;** *(after 'i' or 'h')* **e**
angle-poise lamp **el flexo**
ankle **el tobillo**
another **otro**
answering machine **el**
 contestador automático
antifreeze **el anticongelante**
antique shop **el anticuario**
antiseptic **el antiséptico**
apartment **el apartamento,**
 el piso
aperitif **el aperitivo**
appetite **el apetito**
apple **la manzana**
application form **el impreso**
 de solicitud
appointment
 (business) **la cita;**
 (at hairdresser's) **hora**
apricot **el albaricoque**
April **abril**
are: you are *(informal*
 singular) **eres/estás;**
 (formal singular) **es/está;**
 (informal plural) **sois/**
 estáis; *(formal plural)*
 son/están; *we are* **somos/**
 estamos; *they are*
 son/están
arm **el brazo**
arrive **llegar**
art **el arte**
art gallery **la galería de**
 arte
artichoke **la alcachofa**
artist **el/la artista**
as: as soon as possible
 lo antes posible
ashtray **el cenicero**
asleep: he's asleep
 está dormido
aspirin **la aspirina**
asthmatic **asmático**

at: at the post office **en**
 Correos; *at night* **por la**
 noche; *at 3 o'clock* **a las tres**
Atlantic Ocean
 el Océano Atlántico
ATM **el cajero automático**
attic **el ático**
attractive *(person)* **guapo;**
 (object) **bonito;** *(offer)*
 atractivo
aubergines **las berenjenas**
August **agosto**
aunt **la tía**
Australia **Australia**
Australian **el australiano/**
 la australiana;
 (adj) **australiano**
automatic **automático**
available **disponible**
away: is it far away? **¿está**
 lejos?; *go away!* **¡váyase!**
awful **horrible**
axe **el hacha**
axle **el eje**

B

baby **el niño pequeño,**
 el bebé
baby wipes **las toallitas**
 para bebé
back *(not front)* **la parte de**
 atrás; *(body)* **la espalda**
backpack **la mochila**
bacon **el bacon;** *bacon and*
 eggs **los huevos fritos**
 con bacon
bad **malo**
bag **la bolsa**
bait **el cebo**
bake **cocer al horno**
bakery **la panadería**
balcony **el balcón**
Balearic Islands **las**
 (Islas) Baleares
ball *(football)* **el balon;**
 (tennis etc) **la pelota**

ballpoint pen **el bolígrafo**
banana **el plátano**
band (musicians) **la banda**
bandage **la venda**
bank **el banco**
bank card **la tarjeta de banco**
banknote **el billete de banco**
bar (drinks) **el bar**
barbecue **la barbacoa**
barber **la peluquería de caballeros**
bargain **la ganga**
basement **el sótano**
basin (sink) **el lavabo**
basket **el cesto**
basketball **el baloncesto**
bath **el baño;** *to have a bath* **darse un baño**
bathing suit **el bañador, el traje de baño**
bathroom **el cuarto de baño**
battery (car) **la batería;** (torch etc) **la pila**
Bay of Biscay **el Golfo de Vizcaya**
be **ser/estar**
beach **la playa**
beach ball **el balón de playa**
beans **las judías**
beard **la barba**
beautiful (object) **precioso;** (person) **guapo**
beauty products **los productos de belleza**
because **porque**
bed **la cama**
bed linen **la ropa de cama**
bedroom **el dormitorio**
bedside lamp **la lamparilla de noche**
bedside table **la mesilla de noche**
bedspread **la colcha**
beef **la carne de vaca**
beer **la cerveza**
before ... **antes de ...**
beginner **el/la principiante**
behind ... **detrás de ...**
beige **beige**
bell (church) **la campana;** (door) **el timbre**
below **debajo de**
belt **el cinturón**
beside **al lado de**
best (el) **mejor**
better **mejor**
between **entre**
bicycle **la bicicleta**
big **grande**
bill **la cuenta**
bin **el contenedor de basura**

bin liner **la bolsa de basura**
bird **el pájaro**
birthday **el cumpleaños;** *happy birthday!* **¡felicidades!**
birthday present **el regalo de cumpleaños**
biscuit **la galleta**
bite (by dog) **la mordedura;** (by insect) **la picadura;** (verb: by dog) **morder;** (by insect) **picar**
black **negro**
blackberries **las moras**
blackcurrants **las grosellas negras**
blanket **la manta**
bleach **la lejía;** (verb: hair) **teñir**
blind (cannot see) **ciego**
blinds **las persianas**
blister **la ampolla**
blizzard **la ventisca**
blond(e) (adj) **rubio**
blood **la sangre**
blood test **el análisis de sangre**
blouse **la blusa**
blue **azul**
boarding pass **la tarjeta de embarque**
boat **el barco;** (small) **la barca**
body **el cuerpo**
boil (verb: water) **hervir;** (egg etc) **cocer**
boiled **hervido**
bolt (on door) **el cerrojo;** (verb) **echar el cerrojo**
bone **el hueso**
bonnet (car) **el capó**
book **el libro;** (verb) **reservar**
bookshop **la librería**
boot (footwear) **la bota;** (car) **el maletero**
border **el borde;** (between countries) **la frontera**
boring **aburrido**
born: I was born in ... **nací en ...**
both: both of them **los dos;** *both of us* **los dos;** *both ... and ...* **tanto ... como ...**
bottle **la botella**
bottle opener **el abrebotellas**
bottom **el fondo;** (part of body) **el trasero**
bowl **el cuenco**
box **la caja**
box office **la taquilla**
boy **el chico**
boyfriend **el novio**

bra **el sostén**
bracelet **la pulsera**
braces (clothing) **los tirantes**
brake **el freno;** (verb) **frenar**
branch (of company) **la oficina**
brandy **el coñac**
bread **el pan**
breakdown (car) **la avería;** (nervous) **la crisis nerviosa;** *I've had a breakdown* (car) **he tenido una avería**
breakfast **el desayuno**
breathe **respirar**
bridge **el puente;** (game) **el bridge**
briefcase **la cartera**
British **británico**
brochure **el folleto**
broken **roto**
brooch **el broche**
brother **el hermano**
brown **marrón;** (hair) **castaño;** (skin) **moreno**
bruise **el cardenal**
brush (paint) **la brocha;** (cleaning) **el cepillo;** (hair) **el cepillo del pelo;** (verb: hair) **cepillar el pelo**
budget **el presupuesto**
bucket **el cubo**
builder **el albañil**
building **el edificio**
bull **el toro**
bullfight **la corrida de toros**
bullfighter **el torero**
bullring **la plaza de toros**
bumper **el parachoques**
burglar **el ladrón**
burn **la quemadura;** (verb) **quemar**
bus **el autobús**
business **el negocio;** *it's none of your business* **no es asunto suyo**
business card **la tarjeta de vista**
bus station **la estación de autobuses**
busy (bar) **concurrido;** (engaged) **ocupado**
but **pero**
butcher's **la carnicería**
butter **la mantequilla**
button **el botón**
buy **comprar**
by: by the window **junto a la ventana;** *by Friday* **para el viernes;** *by myself* **yo solo;** *written by* **escrito por**

C

cabbage la col
cable car el teleférico
cable TV la television
  por cable
café el café
cage la jaula
cake (small) el pastel;
  (large) la tarta;
  sponge cake el bizcocho
cake shop la pastelería
calculator la calculadora
call: what's it called?
    ¿cómo se llama?
camcorder la videocámara
camera la máquina de
  fotos, la cámara de fotos
camper van la autocaravana
campfire la hoguera
camping gas el camping-gas
campsite el camping
camshaft el árbol de levas
can (tin) la lata; (verb: to be
  able) poder; can you ...?
  ¿puede ...?; I can't ...
  no puedo ...
Canada Canadá
Canadian canadiense
canal el canal
Canaries las (Islas) Canarias
candle la vela
can opener el abrelatas
cap (bottle) el tapón; (hat)
  la gorra
car el coche
caravan la roulotte
carburetor el carburador
card la tarjeta
cardigan la rebeca
careful prudente;
  be careful! ¡cuidado!
caretaker el portero,
  el encargado
car park el aparcamiento
carpenter el carpintero
carpet la alfombra
carriage (train) el vagón
carrot la zanahoria
car seat (for baby/child)
  el asiento infantil
case (suitcase) la maleta
cash el dinero; cobrar
  (verb); to pay cash pagar
  al contado
cashier el cajero
cashpoint el cajero
  automático
cassette la cassette, la cinta
cassette player el cassette
castanets las castañuelas

Castile Castilla
Castilian castellano
castle el castillo
cat el gato
Catalonia Cataluña
catch (bus etc) coger
cathedral la catedral
Catholic (adj) católico
cauliflower la coliflor
cave la cueva
ceiling el techo
cellar la bodega
cemetery el cementerio
central heating
    la calefacción central
centre el centro
certificate el certificado
chair la silla
change (money) el cambio;
  (verb: money) cambiar;
  (clothes) cambiarse;
  (trains etc) hacer
  transbordo
charger el cargador
check-in (desk)
    la (el mostrador de)
    facturación
check in (verb) facturar
check-out (supermarket)
  la caja
cheers! (toast) ¡salud!
cheese el queso
chemist la farmacia
cheque el cheque
chequebook el talonario
  de cheques
cherry la cereza
chess el ajedrez
chest (part of body) el pecho;
  (furniture) el arcón
chest of drawers la cómoda
chewing gum el chicle
chicken el pollo
child el niño/la niña
children los niños
children's ward
    la sala de pediatría
chimney la chimenea
china la porcelana
chips las patatas fritas
chocolate el chocolate;
  box of chocolates la caja de
  bombones; chocolate bar
  la tableta de chocolate
chop la chuleta;
  (verb: cut) cortar
Christmas la navidad
church la iglesia
cigar el puro
cigarette el cigarrillo
cinema el cine

city la ciudad
city centre el centro
class la clase
classical music
    la música clásica
clean (adj) limpio
cleaner la asistenta
clear (obvious) evidente;
  (water) claro
clever listo
client el cliente
clock el reloj
close (near) cerca; (stuffy)
  sofocante; (verb) cerrar
closed cerrado
clothes la ropa
clubs (cards) tréboles
coat el abrigo
coat hanger la percha
cockroach la cucaracha
cocktail party el coctel
coffee el café
coin la moneda
cold (illness) el resfriado;
  (adj) frío; I have a cold
  tengo un resfriado;
  I'm cold tengo frío
collar el cuello; (of animal)
  el collar
collection (stamps etc)
  la colección; (postal)
  la recogida
colour el color
colour film la película en color
comb el peine; (verb) peinar
come venir; I come from ...
  soy de ...; we came
  last week llegamos
  la semana pasada;
  come here! ¡venga aquí!
come back volver
compact disc
  el disco compacto
compartment
  el compartimento
complicated complicado
computer el ordenador
computer games
  los vídeo-juegos
concert el concierto
conditioner (hair)
  el acondicionador
condom el condón
conductor (bus) el cobrador;
  (orchestra) el director
conference la conferencia
conference room la sala de
  conferencias
congratulations!
¡enhorabuena!
consulate el consulado

contact lenses
  las lentes de contacto
contraceptive el anticonceptivo
contract el contrato
cook el cocinero/la
  cocinera; (verb) guisar
cooker la cocina
cooking utensils los utensilios
  de cocina
cool fresco
cork el corcho
corkscrew el sacacorchos
corner (of street) la esquina;
  (of room) el rincón
corridor el pasillo
cosmetics los cosméticos
cost (verb) costar; what does
  it cost? ¿cuánto cuesta?
cot la cuna
cotton el algodón
cotton wool el algodón
cough la tos; (verb) toser
cough drops las pastillas
  para la garganta
country (state) el país
countryside el campo
cousin el primo/la prima
crab el cangrejo
cramp el calambre
crayfish las cigalas
cream (dairy) la nata;
  (lotion) la crema
credit card la tarjeta
  de crédito
crib el capazo
crisps las patatas fritas
crowded lleno
cruise el crucero
crutches las muletas
cry (weep) llorar;
  (shout) gritar
cucumber el pepino
cuff links los gemelos
cup la taza
cupboard el armario
curlers los rulos
curls los rizos
curry el curry
curtain la cortina
cushion el cojín
customs la aduana
cut la cortadura; (verb) cortar
cycling el ciclismo

D

dad papá
dairy products
  los productos lácteos
damp húmedo
dance el baile; (verb) bailar

dangerous peligroso
dark oscuro; dark blue
  azul oscuro
daughter la hija
day el día
dead muerto
deaf sordo
dear (person) querido
December diciembre
deck of cards la baraja
decorator el pintor
deep profundo
delayed retrasado
deliberately a propósito
delicatessen la charcutería
delivery la entrega
dentist el/la dentista
dentures la dentadura postiza
deny negar
deodorant el desodorante
department el departemento
department store
  los grandes almacenes
departure la salida
departures las salidas
deposit la señal
designer el diseñador/
  la diseñadora
desk la mesa de escritorio
dessert el postre
develop (film) revelar
diabetic diabético
diamonds (jewels) los
  diamantes; (cards)
  los diamantes
diarrhoea la diarrea
diary la agenda
dictionary el
  diccionario
die morir
diesel (oil) fuel-oil;
  (adj: engine) diesel
different diferente; that's
  different! ¡eso es distinto!;
  I'd like a different one
  quisiera otro distinto
difficult difícil
dining room el comedor
dinner la cena
dinner party la cena
dirty sucio
disabled minusválido
discount el descuento
dish cloth el paño de cocina
dishwasher el lavavajillas
disposable nappies los
  pañales desechables
divorced divorciado
do hacer
dock el muelle
doctor el médico/la médica

document el documento
dog el perro
doll la muñeca
dollar el dólar
door la puerta
double room
  la habitación doble
doughnut el dónut
down hacia abajo
drawing pin la chincheta
dress el vestido
drink la bebida; (verb)
  beber; would you like
  something to drink?
  ¿quiere beber algo?
drinking water agua potable
drive (verb) conducir
driver el conductor
driving licence el carnet
  de conducir
drops las gotas
drunk borracho
dry seco; (sherry) fino
dry cleaner la tintorería
during durante
dustbin el cubo de la basura
duster el trapo del polvo
duty-free libre de impuestos;
  duty-free shop el duty-free
duvet el edredón

E

each (every) cada;
  20 euros each
  veinte euros cada uno
ear (inner) el oído; (outer)
  la oreja; ears las orejas
early temprano
earrings los pendientes
east este; the East el Este
easy fácil
eat comer
egg el huevo
eight ocho
eighteen dieciocho
eighty ochenta
either: either of them
  cualquiera de ellos; either
  ... or ... o bien ... o ...
elastic elástico
elbow el codo
electric eléctrico
electrician el/la electricista
electricity la electricidad
eleven once
else: something else algo más;
  someone else alguien más;
  somewhere else en otro sitio
email el email, el correo
  electrónico

email address **la dirección de email**

embarrassing **embarazoso**

embassy **la embajada**

embroidery **el bordado**

emergency **la emergencia**

emergency brake (train) **el freno de emergencia**

emergency department **el servicio de urgencias**

emergency exit **la salida de emergencia**

employee **el empleado**

empty **vacío**

end **el final**

engaged (marriage) **prometido/ prometida;** (telephone) **ocupado**

engine (motor) **el motor**

engineering **la ingeniería**

England **Inglaterra**

English **inglés**

Englishman **el inglés**

Englishwoman **la inglesa**

enlargement **la ampliación**

enough **bastante**

entertainment **las diversiones**

entrance **la entrada**

envelope **el sobre**

epileptic **epiléptico**

eraser **la goma de borrar**

escalator **la escalera mecánica**

especially **sobre todo**

espresso **el café solo**

estimate **el presupuesto**

evening **la tarde**

every **cada;** every day **todos los días**

everyone **todos**

everything **todo**

everywhere **por todas partes**

example **el ejemplo;** for example **por ejemplo**

excellent **excelente**

excess baggage **exceso de equipaje**

exchange (verb) **cambiar**

exchange rate **el cambio**

excursion **la excursión**

excuse me! (to get attention) **¡oiga, por favor!;** (when sneezing etc) **¡perdón!;** excuse me, please (to get past) **¿me hace el favor?**

executive **el ejecutivo**

exhaust **el tubo de escape**

exhibition **la exposición**

exit **la salida**

expensive **caro**

extension cord **el cable alargador**

eye **el ojo**

eyebrow **la ceja**

F

face **la cara**

faint (unclear) **tenue;** (verb) **desmayarse;** I feel faint **estoy mareado**

fair **la feria;** it's not fair **no hay derecho**

false teeth **la dentadura postiza**

family **la familia**

fan (enthusiast) **el fan;** (football) **el hincha;** (ventilator) **el ventilador;** (handheld) **el abanico**

fantastic **fantástico**

far **lejos;** how far is it to ...? **¿qué distancia hay a ...?**

fare **el billete, la tarifa**

farm **la granja**

farmer **el granjero**

fashion **la moda**

fast **rápido**

fat (adj) **gordo;** (on meat) **la grasa**

father **el padre**

fax **el fax;** (verb) **enviar por fax**

February **febrero**

feel (touch) **tocar;** I feel hot **tengo calor;** I feel like ... **me apetece ...;** I don't feel well **no me encuentro bien**

felt-tip pen **el rotulador**

fence **la cerca**

ferry **el ferry**

fiancé **el prometido**

fiancée **la prometida**

field (of grass etc) **el campo;** (of study) **la especialidad**

fifteen **quinze**

fifty **cincuenta**

fig **el higo**

figures **los números**

filling (in tooth) **el empaste;** (in sandwich, cake) **el relleno**

film **la película**

filter **el filtro**

filter papers **los papeles de filtro**

finger **el dedo**

fire **el fuego;** (blaze) **el incendio**

fire extinguisher **el extintor**

fireplace **la chimenea**

fireworks **los fuegos artificiales**

first **primero;** first aid **primeros auxilios**

first class **de primera**

first floor **el primer piso**

first name **el nombre de pila**

fish **el pez;** (food) **el pescado**

fishing **la pesca;** to go fishing **ir a pescar**

fishmonger's **la pescadería**

five **cinco**

fizzy water **el agua con gas**

flag **la bandera**

flash (camera) **el flash**

flat (level) **plano**

flat tyre **la rueda pinchada**

flavour **el sabor**

flea **la pulga**

flea spray **el spray antipulgas**

flight **el vuelo**

floor **el suelo;** (storey) **el piso**

flour **la harina**

flower **la flor**

flowerbed **el parterre**

flute **la flauta**

fly (insect) **la mosca;** (verb: of plane, insect) **volar;** (of person) **viajar en avión**

flyover **el paso elevado**

fog **la niebla**

folk music **la música folklórica**

food **la comida**

food poisoning **la intoxicación alimenticia**

foot **el pie**

football **el fútbol;** (ball) **el balón**

for: for me **para mí;** what for? **¿para qué?;** for a week **(para) una semana**

foreigner **el extranjero/ la extranjera**

forest **el bosque;** (tropical) **la selva**

forget **olvidar**

fork **el tenedor;** (garden) **la horca**

forty **cuarenta**

fountain **la fuente**

fountain pen **la (pluma) estilográfica**

four **cuatro**

fourteen **catorce**

fourth **cuarto**

France **Francia**
free (not engaged) **libre**;
 (no charge) **gratis**
freezer **el congelador**
French **francés**
Friday **viernes**
fridge **el frigorífico**
fried **frito**
friend **el amigo/la amiga**
friendly **simpático**
fringe (hair) **el flequillo**
front: in front of ...
 delante de ...
frost **la escarcha**
frozen foods **los congelados**
fruit **la fruta**
fruit juice **el zumo de frutas**
fry **freír**
frying pan **la sartén**
full **lleno**; I'm full
 (up) **estoy lleno**
full board **pensión completa**
funny **divertido**; (odd) **raro**
furniture **los muebles**

G

garage (for parking) **el garage**;
 (for repairs) **el taller**
garden **el jardín**
garden centre **el vivero**
garlic **el ajo**
gas-permeable lenses
 **las lentes de contacto
 semi-rígidas**
gate **la puerta, la verja**;
 (at airport) **la puerta
 de embarque**
gay (homosexual) **gay**
gearbox **la caja de cambios**
gear stick **la palanca
 de velocidades**
gel (hair) **el gel**
German **alemán**
Germany **Alemania**
get (fetch) **traer**; have you
 got ...? **¿tiene ...?**; to get
 the train **coger el tren**
get back: we get back tomorrow
 nos volvemos mañana;
 to get something back
 recobrar algo
get in (of train etc) **subirse**;
 (of person) **llegar**
get off (bus etc) **bajarse**
get on (bus etc) **subirse**
get out **bajarse**;
 (bring out) **sacar**
get up (rise) **levantarse**
Gibraltar **Gibraltar**
gift **el regalo**

gin **la ginebra**
ginger (spice) **el jengibre**
girl **la chica**
girlfriend **la novia**
give **dar**
glad **alegre**
glass (material) **el cristal**;
 (for drinking) **el vaso,
 la copa**
glasses **las gafas**
gloss prints **las copias
 con brillo**
gloves **los guantes**
glue **el pegamento**
go **ir**
gold **el oro**
good **bueno**; good! **¡bien!**
good afternoon **buenas tardes**
goodbye **adiós**
good evening **buenas noches**
good morning **buenos días**
government **el gobierno**
granddaughter **la nieta**
grandfather **el abuelo**
grandmother **la abuela**
grandparents **los abuelos**
grandson **el nieto**
grapes **las uvas**
grass **la hierba**
Great Britain **Gran Bretaña**
green **verde**
greengrocer's **la verdulería**
grey **gris**
grill **la parrilla**
grilled **a la plancha**
grocer's **el ultramarinos,
 la tienda de comestibles**
ground floor **la planta baja**
groundsheet **la lona
 impermeable,
 el suelo aislante**
guarantee **la garantía**;
 (verb) **garantizar**
guest **la invitada**
guide **el/la guía**
guide book **la guía turística**
guided tour **la visita con guía**
guitar **la guitarra**
gun (rifle) **la escopeta**;
 (pistol) **la pistola**

H

hair **el pelo**
haircut **el corte de pelo**
hairdresser's **la peluquería**
hairdryer **el secador** (de pelo)
hairspray **la laca**
half **medio**;
 half an hour **media hora**
half board **media pensión**

ham **el jamón**
hamburger **la hamburguesa**
hammer **el martillo**
hamster **el hámster**
hand **la mano**
handbag **el bolso**
handbrake **el freno de mano**
handle (door) **el picaporte**
hand luggage
 el equipaje de mano
handshake
 el apretón de manos
handsome **guapo**
hangover **la resaca**
happy **contento, feliz**
harbour **el puerto**
hard **duro**; (difficult) **difícil**
hardware store **la ferretería**
hat **el sombrero**;
 (woollen) **el gorro**
have **tener**; I don't have ... **no
 tengo ...**; do you have ...?
 ¿tiene ...?; I have to go
 tengo que irme ; can I
 have ...? **¿me pone ...?**
hay fever **la fiebre del heno**
he **él**
head **la cabeza**
headache **el dolor de cabeza**
headlights **los faros**
headphones **los auriculares**
hear **oír**
hearing aid **el audífono**
heart **el corazón**
hearts (cards) **los corazones**
heater **la estufa**
heating **la calefacción**
heavy **pesado**
hedge **el seto**
heel **el talón**; (shoe) **el tacón**
hello **hola**; (on phone)
 dígame
help **la ayuda**; (verb) **ayudar**
hepatitis **la hepatitis**
her: it's for her **es para ella**;
 her book **su libro**; her shoes
 sus zapatos; it's hers **es
 suyo**; give it to her **déselo**
high **alto**
highway code **el código
 de la circulación**
hiking **el senderismo**
hill **el monte**
him: it's for him **es para él**;
 give it to him **déselo**
hire (verb) **alquilar**
his: his book **su libro**; his shoes
 sus zapatos; it's his **es suyo**
history **la historia**
hitchhike **hacer auto-stop**
HIV positive **seropositivo**

hobby **el hobby**
holiday **las vacaciones**
home **la casa;**
　at home **en casa**
homeopathy **la homeopatía**
honest **honrado;**
　(sincere) **sincero**
honey **la miel**
honeymoon **el viaje de novios**
horn (car) **el claxon;** (animal)
el cuerno
horrible **horrible**
hospital **el hospital**
hostess **la anfitriona**
hour **la hora**
house **la casa**
household products **los**
　productos del hogar
hovercraft **el aerodeslizador**
how? **¿cómo?**
how are you? **¿qué tal?**
hundred **cien**
hungry: I'm hungry
　tengo hambre
hurry: I'm in a hurry
　tengo prisa
husband **el marido**
hydrofoil **la hidroaleta**

I
I **yo**
ice **el hielo**
ice cream **el helado**
ice skates
　los patines para hielo
if **si**
ignition **el encendido**
immediately **inmediatamente**
impossible **imposible**
in **en;** in English **en inglés;** in
　the hotel **en el hotel;** in
　Barcelona **en Barcelona;**
　he's not in **no está**
included **incluido**
indicator **el intermitente**
indigestion **indigestión**
inexpensive **barato**
infection **la infección**
information **la información**
inhaler (for asthma etc)
　el spray, el inhalador
injection **la inyección**
injury **la herida**
ink **la tinta**
inn **la fonda**
inner tube
　la cámara (neumática)
insect **el insecto**
insect repellent
　la loción anti-mosquitos

insomnia **el insomnio**
instant coffee
　el café instantáneo
insurance **el seguro**
interesting **interesante**
internet **el internet**
interpret **interpretar**
interpreter **el/la intérprete**
invitation **la invitación**
invoice **la factura**
Ireland **Irlanda**
Irish **irlandés/ irlandesa**
iron (metal) **el hierro;**
　(for clothes) **la plancha;**
　(verb) **planchar**
is **es/está**
island **la isla**
it **lo/la**
Italian (adj) **italiano/
　italiana** (m/f)
Italy **Italia**
its **su**

J
jacket **la chaqueta**
jam **la mermelada**
January **enero**
jazz **el jazz**
jeans **los tejanos,
　los vaqueros**
jellyfish **la medusa**
jeweller's **la joyería**
job **el trabajo**
jog (verb) **hacer footing**
joke **la broma;**
　(funny story) **el chiste**
journey **el viaje**
juice **el zumo**
July **julio**
June **junio**
just (only) **sólo;** it's just arrived
　acaba de llegar

K
kettle **el hervidor de agua**
key **la llave**
keyboard **el teclado**
kidney **el riñón**
kilo **el kilo**
kilometre **el kilómetro**
kitchen **la cocina**
knee **la rodilla**
knife **el cuchillo**
knit **hacer punto**
knitwear
　los artículos de punto
know **saber;** (person,
　place) **conocer;**
　I don't know **no sé**

L
label **la etiqueta**
lace **el encaje**
laces (shoe) **los cordones**
　(de los zapatos)
lady **la señora**
lake **el lago**
lamb **el cordero**
lamp **la lámpara, el flexo**
lampshade **la pantalla**
land **la tierra;**
　(verb) **aterrizar**
language **el idioma**
large **grande**
last (final) **último;**
　at last! **¡por fin! ;** last week
　la semana pasada
late: it's getting late **se está
　haciendo tarde;** the bus is
　late **el autobús se
　ha retrasado**
later **más tarde**
laugh **reír**
laundrette **la lavandería
　automática**
laundry (dirty) **la ropa sucia;**
　(washed) **la colada**
law **el derecho**
lawn **el césped**
lawn mower **la maquina
　cortacésped**
lawyer **el abogado/
　la abogada**
laxative **el laxante**
lazy **perezoso**
lead **la correa**
leaf **la hoja**
leaflet **el folleto**
learn **aprender**
leather **el cuero**
lecture theatre **el anfiteatro**
lecturer (university)
　**el profesor/la profesora
　de universidad**
left (not right) **izquierdo;**
　there's nothing left
　no queda nada
leg **la pierna**
lemon **el limón**
lemonade **la limonada**
length **la longitud**
lens **la lente**
less **menos**
lesson **la clase**
letter (mail) **la carta;**
　(of alphabet) **la letra**
lettuce **la lechuga**
library **la biblioteca**
licence **el permiso**
life **la vida**

lift **el ascensor**
light **la luz;** (weight)
  ligero; (not dark) **claro**
light bulb **la bombilla**
lighter **el encendedor**
lighter fuel **el gas para
  el encendedor**
light meter **el fotómetro**
like: I like … **me gusta …;** I like
  swimming **me gusta
  nadar;** it's like … **es
  como …;** like this one
como éste
lime (fruit) **la lima**
line **la cola;** (phone etc)
  línea; (verb) **hacer cola**
lipstick **la barra de labios**
liqueur **el licor**
list **la lista**
literature **la literatura**
litre **el litro**
litter **la basura**
little (small) **pequeño;** it's a
  little big **es un poco
  grande;** just a little **sólo
  un poquito**
liver **el hígado**
living room **el cuarto de estar**
lobster **la langosta**
lollipop **el chupa-chups**
long **largo**
lost property office **la oficina
  de objetos perdidos**
lot: a lot **mucho**
loud **alto**
lounge (in house)
  el cuarto de estar;
  (in hotel etc) **el salón**
love **el amor;** (verb) **querer;**
  I love Spain **me
  encanta España**
lover **el/la amante**
low **bajo**
luck: good luck! **¡suerte!**
luggage **el equipaje**
luggage rack **la rejilla
  de equipajes**
lunch **la comida**

M

mad **loco**
madam **señora**
magazine **la revista**
mail **el correo**
main course **el plato principal**
main road **la calle principal**
Majorca **Mallorca**
make **hacer**
make-up **el maquillaje**
man **el hombre**

manager **el/la gerente,
  el jefe;** (hotel)
  el director/la directora
many **muchos/muchas;**
  many thanks **muchas
  gracias;** many people
  mucha gente; how many
  ¿cuántos?; too many
  demasiados; not many
  no muchos
map **el mapa;**
  town map/plan **el plano**
marble **el mármol**
March **marzo**
margarine **la margarina**
market **el mercado**
marmalade **la mermelada
  de naranja**
married **casado**
mascara **el rímel**
mass (church) **la misa**
match (light) **la cerilla;**
  (sport) **el partido**
material (cloth) **la tela**
matter: it doesn't matter
  no importa
mattress **el colchón**
May **mayo**
maybe **quizás**
me: it's for me **es para mí;**
  give it to me **démelo**
meal **la comida**
mean: what does this mean?
  ¿qué significa esto?
meat **la carne**
mechanic **el mecánico**
medicine **la medicina**
Mediterranean
  el Mediterráneo
medium (sherry) **amontillado**
medium-dry (wine) **semi-seco**
meeting **la reunión**
melon **el melón**
menu **la carta;** set menu
  el menú (del día)
message **el recado,
  el mensaje**
metro station
  le estación de metro
microwave **el microondas**
midday **el mediodía**
middle: in the middle
  en el centro
midnight **medianoche**
milk **la leche**
mine: it's mine **es mío**
mineral water
  el agua mineral
minute **el minuto**
mirror **el espejo**
Miss **Señorita**

mistake **la equivocación**
mobile phone
  **el teléfono móvil,
  el teléfono celular**
modem **el modem**
Monday **lunes**
money **el dinero**
monitor **el monitor**
month **el mes**
monument **el monumento**
moon **la luna**
moped **el ciclomotor**
more **más**
morning **la mañana;**
  in the morning
  por la mañana
Morocco **Marruecos**
mosaic **el mosaico**
mosquito **el mosquito**
mother **la madre**
motorboat **la motora**
motorcycle **la motocicleta**
motorway **la autopista**
mountain **la montaña**
mountain bike
  la bicicleta de montaña
mouse **el ratón**
mousse (for hair)
  **la espuma
  moldeadora**
moustache **el bigote**
mouth **la boca**
move (verb: something)
  mover; (oneself)
  moverse; (house)
  mudarse de casa;
  don't move! **¡no se mueva!**
movie **la película**
Mr **Señor**
Mrs **Señora**
much: much better **mucho
  mejor;** much slower **mucho
  más despacio**
mug **la jarrita**
Mum **mama**
museum **el museo**
mushrooms **los
  champiñones, las setas**
music **la música**
musical instrument
  el instrumento musical
musician **el músico**
music system **el equipo
  de música**
mussels **los mejillones**
must (to have to) **tener que**
  I must … **tengo que …**
mustard **la mostaza**
my: my book **mi libro;**
  my keys **mis llaves**

N

nail (metal) el clavo;
(finger) la uña
nail clippers el cortauñas
nailfile la lima de uñas
nail polish el esmalte
de uñas
name el nombre; what's your
name? ¿cómo se llama
usted?; my name is...
me llamo...
napkin la servilleta
nappy el pañal
narrow estrecho
near: near the door junto a
la puerta; near New York
cerca de New York
necessary necesario
neck el cuello
necklace el collar
need (verb) necesitar;
I need ... necesito ...; there's
no need no hace falta
needle la aguja
negative (photo) el negativo
neither: neither of them
ninguno de ellos; neither ...
nor ... ni ... ni ...
nephew el sobrino
never nunca
new nuevo
news las noticias
newsagent's el kiosko
de periódicos
newspaper el periódico
New Zealand Nueva Zelanda
New Zealander
el neozelandés/
la neozelandesa
next próximo, siguiente;
next week la semana que
viene; what next?
¿y ahora qué?
nice bonito; (pleasant)
agradable; (to eat) bueno
niece la sobrina
night la noche
nightclub la discoteca
nightgown el camisón
night porter
el vigilante nocturno
nine nueve
nineteen diecinueve
ninety noventa
no (response) no; I have no
money no tengo dinero
nobody nadie
noisy ruidoso
noon mediodía
north el norte

Northern Ireland
Irlanda del Norte
nose la nariz
not no; he's not ... no es/está ...
notebook el cuaderno
notepad el bloc
nothing nada
novel la novela
November noviembre
now ahora
nowhere en ninguna parte
nudist el/la nudista
number el número
number plate la matrícula
nurse el enfermo/la
enferma
nut (fruit) la nuez;
(for bolt) la tuerca

O

oars los remos
occasionally de vez en cuando
occupied ocupado
October octubre
octopus el pulpo
of de
office (place) la oficina;
(room) el despacho
office block el bloque
de oficinas
often a menudo
oil el aceite
ointment la pomada
OK vale
old viejo; how old are you?
¿cuántos años tiene?
olive la aceituna
olive oil el aceite de oliva
olive tree el olivo
omelette la tortilla
on ... en ...
one uno
onion la cebolla
only sólo
open (adj) abierto;
(verb) abrir
opening times el horario
de apertura
operating theatre el quirófano
operation la operación
operator la operadora
opposite: opposite the hotel
enfrente del hotel
optician el/la oculista
or o
orange (fruit) la naranja;
(colour) naranja
orchestra la orquesta
order el pedido
organ (music) el órgano

other: the other (one) el otro
our nuestro; it's ours
es nuestro
out: he's out no está
outside fuera; external externa
oven el horno
over ... encima de ...; (more
than) más de ...; it's over
the road está al otro lado
de la calle; when the party
is over cuando termine
la fiesta; over there allí
overtake (in car) adelantar
oyster la ostra

P

package el paquete
packet el paquete;
(cigarettes) la cajetilla;
(sweets, crisps)
la bolsa
padlock el candado
page la página
pain el dolor
paint la pintura
pair el par
palace el palacio
pale pálido
pancakes las crepes
paper el papel;
(newspaper) el periódico
paraffin la parafina
parcel el paquete
pardon? ¿cómo dice?
parents los padres
park el parque; (verb)
aparcar; no parking
prohibido aparcar
parsley el perejil
parting (hair) la raya
party (celebration) la fiesta;
(group) el grupo;
(political) el partido
passenger el pasajero
passport el pasaporte
password la contraseña
pasta la pasta
path el camino
pavement la acera
pay pagar
payment el pago
peach el melocotón
peanuts los cacahuetes
pear la pera
pearl la perla
peas los guisantes
pedestrian el peatón
pedestrian zone la zona
peatonal
peg la pinza

pen **la pluma**
pencil **el lápiz**
pencil sharpener **el sacapuntas**
penknife **la navaja**
pen pal **el amigo/la amiga
por correspondencia**
people **la gente**
pepper **la pimienta;**
(red, green) **el pimiento**
peppermints **las pastillas
de menta**
per: per night **por noche**
perfect **perfecto**
perfume **el perfume**
perhaps **quizás**
perm **la permanente**
pet passport **el pasaporte
de animales**
petrol **la gasolina**
petrol station **la gasolinera**
pets **los animales
de compañía; los
animales domésticos**
phone book **la guía telefónica**
phone booth **la cabina
telefónica**
phonecard **la tarjeta telefónica**
photocopier **la fotocopiadora**
photograph **la foto** (grafía);
(verb) **fotografiar**
photographer **el fotógrafo**
phrase book **el libro de frases**
piano **el piano**
pickpocket **el carterista**
picnic **el picnic**
piece **el pedazo**
pill **la pastilla**
pillow **la almohada**
pilot **el piloto**
PIN **el pin**
pin **el alfiler**
pine (tree) **el pino**
pineapple **la piña**
pink **rosa**
pipe (for smoking) **la pipa;**
(for water) **la tubería**
piston **el piston**
pitch **la plaza**
pizza **la pizza**
place **el lugar;** at your place
en su casa
plant **la planta**
plaster **la tirita**
plastic **el plástico**
plastic bag **la bolsa de plástico**
plastic wrap **el plástico
para envolver**
plate **el plato**
platform (train) **el andén**
play (theatre) **la obra
de teatro;** (verb) **jugar**

please **por favor**
pleased to meet you
encantado/encantada
plug (electrical) **el enchufe;**
(sink) **el tapón**
plumber **el fontanero/
la fontenera**
pocket **el bolsillo**
poison **el veneno**
police **la policía**
police officer **el policía**
police report **la denuncia**
police station **la comisaría**
politics **la política**
poor **pobre;** (bad quality)
malo
pop music **la música pop**
pork **la carne de cerdo**
port (harbour) **el puerto;**
(drink) **el oporto**
porter (hotel) **el conserje**
Portugal **Portugal**
Portuguese **portugués**
possible **posible**
post **el correo;** (verb) **echar
al correo**
postbox **el buzón**
postcard **la postal**
postcode **el código postal**
poster **el póster**
postman **el cartero**
post office (la oficina de)
Correos
potato **la patata**
poultry **las aves**
pound (sterling) **la libra**
powder **el polvo;**
(cosmetic) **los polvos**
pram **el cochecito**
prawns **las gambas**
prefer **preferir**
pregnant **embarazada**
prescription **la receta**
pretty **bonito;** (quite) **bastante**
price **el precio**
priest **el cura**
printer **la impresora**
private **privado**
problem **el problema**
profession **la profesión**
professor **el catedrático**
profits **los beneficios**
prohibited **prohibido**
protection factor (SPF) **el
factor de protección**
public **público**
public holiday **el día de
fiesta**
public swimming pool
la piscina municipal
pull **tirar de**

puncture **el pinchazo**
purple **morado**
purse **la cartera,
el monedero**
push **empujar**
pushchair **la sillita de ruedas**
put **poner**
pyjamas **el pijama**
Pyrenees **los Pirineos**

Q

quality **la calidad**
quarter **el cuarto**
question **la pregunta**
quick **rápido**
quiet **tranquilo;**
(person) **callado**
quite (fairly) **bastante;**
(fully) **completamente**

R

rabbit **el conejo**
radiator **el radiador**
radio **la radio**
radish **el rábano**
rake **el rastrillo**
railway **el ferrocarril**
rain **la lluvia**
raincoat **la gabardina**
rainforest **la selva**
raisins **las pasas**
raspberry **la frambuesa**
rare (uncommon) **raro;**
(steak) **poco hecho,
poco pasado**
rat **la rata**
razor blades
las cuchillas de afeitar
read **leer**
ready **listo**
ready meals
los platos preparados
receipt **el recibo**
reception **la recepción**
receptionist **el/
la recepcionista**
record (music) **el disco;**
(sport etc) **el récord**
record player **el tocadiscos**
record store **la tienda de discos**
red **rojo;** (wine) **tinto**
refreshments **los refrescos**
refrigerator **el frigorífico**
registered post
correo certificado
relative **el pariente**
relax **relajarse;** (rest)
descansar
religion **la religión**

remember: I remember
  me acuerdo; I don't
  remember **no me acuerdo**
repair **arreglar**
report **el informe**
reservation **la reserva**
rest (remainder) **el resto;**
  (verb: relax) **descansar**
restaurant **el restaurante**
restaurant car
  el vagón-restaurante
return (come back) **volver;**
  (give back) **devolver**
return ticket **el billete**
  de ida y vuelta
rice **el arroz**
rich **rico**
right (correct) **correcto;**
  (not left) **derecho**
ring (for finger) **el anillo**
ripe **maduro**
river **el río**
road **la carretera**
roasted **asado**
robbery **el robo**
rock (stone) **la roca**
roll (bread) **el bollo**
roof **el tejado**
room **la habitación;** (space)
  el sitio
room service **el servicio**
  de habitaciones
rope **la cuerda**
rose **la rosa**
round (circular) **redondo**
roundabout **la rotonda**
row (verb) **remar**
rowing boat **la barca de remos**
rubber (material) **la goma**
rubber band **la goma**
rubbish **la basura**
ruby (stone) **el rubí**
rug (mat) **la alfombra;**
  (blanket) **la manta**
rugby **el rugby**
ruins **las ruinas**
ruler (for measuring) **la regla**
rum **el ron**
run (**verb**) **correr**
runway **la pista**

S

sad **triste**
safe (not dangerous)
  seguro
safety pin **el imperdible**
sailboard **la tabla**
  de windsurfing
sailing **la vela**
salad **la ensalada**

sale (at reduced prices)
  las rebajas
sales **las ventas**
salmon **el salmón**
salt **la sal**
same: the same dress **el**
  mismo vestido; the same
  people **la misma gente;**
  same again, please **lo**
  mismo otra vez, por favor
sand **la arena**
sandals **las sandalias**
sand dunes **las dunas**
sandwich **el bocadillo**
sanitary towels **las compresas**
Saturday **sábado**
sauce **la salsa**
saucepan **el cazo**
saucer **el platillo**
sauna **la sauna**
sausage **la salchicha**
say **decir;** what did you
  say? **¿qué ha dicho?;**
  how do you say ...?
  ¿cómo se dice ...?
scampi **las gambas**
scarf **la bufanda;** (head)
  el pañuelo
schedule **el programa**
school **la escuela**
science **las ciencias**
scissors **las tijeras**
Scotland **Escocia**
Scottish **escocés/escocesa**
screen **la pantalla**
screw **el tornillo**
screwdriver **el destornillador**
sea **el mar**
seafood **los mariscos**
seat **el asiento**
seat belt **el cinturón**
  de seguridad
second **el segundo**
second class **de segunda**
see **ver;** I can't see **no veo;**
  I see **comprendo**
self-employed (person) **el**
  autónomo/la autónoma
sell **vender**
seminar **el seminario**
send **mandar**
separate (adj) **distinto**
separated **separado**
September **septiembre**
serious **serio**
seven **siete**
seventeen **diecisiete**
seventy **setenta**
several **varios**
sew **coser**
shampoo **el champú**

shave **el afeitado;**
  to have a shave **afeitarse**
shaving foam **la espuma**
  de afeitar
shawl **el chal**
she **ella**
sheet **la sábana;** (of paper)
  la hoja
shell **la concha**
shellfish **mariscos**
sherry **el jerez**
ship **el barco**
shirt **la camisa**
shoelaces **los cordones**
  de los zapatos
shoe polish **la crema**
  de zapatos
shoes **los zapatos**
shoe shop **la zapatería**
shop **la tienda**
shopping **la compra;** to go
  shopping **ir de compras**
short **corto;** (height) **bajo**
shorts **los pantalones cortos**
shoulder **el hombro**
shower (bath) **la ducha;**
  (rain) **el chaparrón**
shower gel **el gel de ducha**
shrimp **las quisquillas**
shutter (camera)
  el obturador; (window)
  el postigo
sick: I feel sick **tengo náuseas;**
  to be sick (vomit) **devolver**
side (edge) **el borde**
side lights **las luces**
  de posición
sights: the sights of ... **los**
  lugares de interés de ...
sightseeing **el turismo**
silk **la seda**
silver (metal) **la plata;**
  (colour) **plateado**
simple **sencillo**
sing **cantar**
single (ticket) **de ida;**
  (only) **único;** (unmarried)
  soltero/soltera
single room
  la habitación individual
sink **el fregadero**
sister **la hermana**
six **seis**
sixteen **dieciséis**
sixty **sesenta**
skid **patinar**
skiing: to go skiing **ir a esquiar**
skin cleanser
  la leche limpiadora
ski resort **la estación**
  de esquí

skirt **la falda**
skis **los esquís**
sky **el cielo**
sleep **el sueño**; (verb) **dormir**
sleeper car **el coche-cama**
sleeping bag **el saco de dormir**
sleeping pill **el somnífero**
sleeve **la manga**
slip (underwear)
   la combinacíon
slippers **las zapatillas**
slow **lento**
small **pequeño**
smell **el olor**; (verb) **oler**
smile **la sonrisa**;
   (verb) **sonreír**
smoke **el humo**; (verb) **fumar**
snack **la comida ligera**
snow **la nieve**
so: so good **tan bueno**;
   not so much **no tanto**
soaking solution
   (for contact lenses)
   la solución limpiadora
soap **el jabón**
socks **los calcetines**
soda water **la soda**
sofa **el sofa**
soft **blando**
soil **la tierra**
somebody **alguien**
somehow **de algún modo**
something **algo**
sometimes **a veces**
somewhere **en alguna parte**
son **el hijo**
song **la canción**
sorry! **¡perdón!**; I'm sorry
   perdón/lo siento; sorry?
   (pardon) **¿cómo dice?**
soup **la sopa**
south **el sur**
South America **Sudamérica**
souvenir **el recuerdo**
spade **la pala**
spades (cards) **las picas**
Spain **España**
Spaniard **el español/**
   la española
speak **hablar**;
   do you speak ...? **¿habla ...?**;
   I don't speak ... **no hablo ...**
speed **la velocidad**
speed limit **el límite de**
velocidad
spider **la araña**
spinach **las espinacas**
spoon **la cuchara**
sport **el deporte**
sports centre
   el centro deportivo

spring (mechanical) **el muelle**;
   (season) **la primavera**
square (in town) **la plaza**;
   (adj) **cuadrado**
staircase **la escalera**
stairs **las escaleras**
stamp **el sello**
stapler **la grapadora**
star **la estrella**
start (beginning) **el**
   principio; (verb) **empezar**
starters **los entrantes**
statement **la declaración**
station **la estación**
statue **la estatua**
steak **el filete**
steal **robar**; it's been stolen
   lo han robado
steamed **al vapor**
steamer (boat) **el vapor**
stepdaughter **la hijastra**
stepfather **el padastro**
stepmother **la madastra**
stepson **el hijastro**
still water **el agua sin gas**
stockings **las medias**
stomach **el estómago**
stomach-ache **el dolor**
   de estómago
stop (bus) **la parada**; (verb)
   parar; stop! **¡alto!**
storm **la tormenta**
strawberries **las fresas**
stream (small river) **el arroyo**
street **la calle**
string **la cuerda**
stroller **la sillita de ruedas**
strong **fuerte**
student **el/la estudiante**
stupid **estúpido**
suburbs **las afueras**
sugar **el azúcar**
suit (clothing) **el traje**;
   it suits you **te sienta bien**
suitcase **la maleta**
sun **el sol**
sunbathe **tomar el sol**
sunburn **la quemadura de sol**
Sunday **domingo**
sunglasses **las gafas de sol**
sunny: it's sunny **hace sol**
sunshade **la sombrilla**
sunstroke **la insolación**
suntan: to get a suntan
   broncearse
suntan lotion
   la loción bronceadora
suntanned **bronceado**
supermarket **el supermercado**
supper **la cena**
supplement **el suplemento**

suppository **el supositorio**
sure **seguro**
surname **el apellido**
sweat **el sudor**; (verb) **sudar**
sweater **el jersey**
sweatshirt **la sudadera**
sweet (adj: not sour) **dulce**;
   sweets **los caramelos** (m)
swim (verb) **nadar**
swimming **la natación**
swimming pool **la piscina**
swimming trunks **el bañador**
switch **el interruptor**
synagogue **la sinagoga**
syringe **la jeringuilla**
syrup **el jarabe**

T

table **la mesa**
tablet **la pastilla**
take **tomar**
take off **el despegue**
talcum powder
   los polvos de talco
talk **la charla**; (verb) **hablar**
tall **alto**
tampons **los tampones**
tangerine **la mandarina**
tap **el grifo**
tapestry **el tapiz**
taxi **el taxi**
taxi rank **la parada de** taxis
tea **el té**
teacher **el profesor/**
   la profesora
technician **el técnico**
telephone **el teléfono**; (verb)
   llamar por teléfono
television la **televisión**
temperature **la temperatura**;
   (fever) **la fiebre**
ten **diez**
tennis **el tenis**
tent **la tienda** (de campaña)
tent peg
   la estaquilla, la estaca
tent pole **el mástil**
terminal **la terminal**
terrace **la terraza**
test **la prueba**
than **que**
thank (verb) **agradecer**;
   thank you/thanks **gracias**;
that **ese/esa, eso**;
   that bus **ese autobús**;
   that man **ese hombre**;
   that woman **esa mujer**;
   what's that? **¿qué es eso?**;
   I think that ... **creo que ...**;
   that one **ése/ésa**

the **el/la;** (plural) **los/las**
theatre **el teatro**
their: their room **su
    habitación;** their books **sus
    libros;** it's theirs **es suyo**
them: it's for them
    es para ellos/ellas;
    give it to them **déselo**
then **entonces;** (after)
    después
there **allí;** there is/are ... **hay ...;**
    is/are there ...? **¿hay ...?**
these: these men
estos hombres; these women
    estas mujeres; these are
    mine **éstos son míos**
they **ellos/ellas**
thick **grueso**
thief **el ladrón**
thin **delgado**
think **pensar;**
    I think so **creo que sí;**
    I'll think about it **lo pensaré**
third **tercero**
thirsty: I'm thirsty **tengo sed**
thirteen **trece**
thirty **treinta**
this: this one **éste/ésta;**
    this man **este hombre;**
    this woman **esta mujer;**
    what's this? **¿qué es esto?;**
    this is Mr ... **éste es
    el señor ...**
those: those men **esos
hombres;** those women
    esas mujeres
thousand **mil**
throat **la garganta**
through **por**
three **tres**
thunderstorm **la tormenta**
Thursday **jueves**
ticket (train etc) **el billete;**
    (theatre etc) **la entrada**
ticket office **la taquilla**
tide **la marea**
tie **la corbata;** (verb) **atar**
tight **ajustado**
tights **las medias, los pantis**
time **tiempo;** what's the time?
    ¿qué hora es?
timetable **el horario**
tin **la hojalata**
tip (end) **la punta;** (money)
    la propina
tired **cansado**
tissues **los pañuelos de papel**
to: to America **a América;** to
    the station **a la estación;** to
    the doctor **al médico**
toast **la tostada**

tobacco **el tabaco**
tobacconist **el estanco**
today **hoy**
together **juntos**
toilet (room in house) **el
    baño;** (bathroom item)
    el váter; (in public
    establishment) **los
    servicos**
toilet paper **el papel higiénico**
toilets (men) **los servicios
    de caballeros;** (women)
    los servicios de señoras
tomato **el tomate**
tomato juice **el zumo
    de tomate**
tomorrow **mañana**
tongue **la lengua**
tonic **la tónica**
tonight **esta noche**
too (also) **también;**
    (excessively) **demasiado**
tooth **el diente;**
    back tooth **la muela**
toothache **el dolor de muelas**
toothbrush **el cepillo
    de dientes**
toothpaste **la pasta dentífrica**
torch **la linterna**
tour **la excursión**
tourist **el/la turista**
tourist office
    la oficina de turismo
towel **la toalla**
tower **la torre**
town **el pueblo**
town hall **el ayuntamiento**
toy **el juguete**
trade fair **la feria**
track suit **el chandal**
tractor **el tractor**
tradition **la tradición**
traffic **el tráfico**
traffic jam **el atasco**
traffic lights **el semáforo**
trailer **la caravana,
    el remolque**
train **el tren**
trainee **el aprendiz**
trainers **los zapatos
    de deporte**
translate **traducir**
translator **el traductor/
    la traductora**
travel agency **la agencia
    de viajes**
traveller's cheque
    el cheque de viaje
tray **la bandeja**
tree **el árbol**
trolley **el carrito**

trousers **el pantalón**
truck **el camión**
true **cierto;** it's true **es verdad**
try **intentar**
Tuesday **martes**
tunnel **el túnel**
turn (left/right) **tuerza
    (a la izquierda/ a
    la derecha)**
turn: it's my turn **me toca
    a mí**
tweezers **las pinzas**
twelve **doce**
twenty **veinte**
two **dos**
typewriter **la máquina
    de escribir**
tyre **el neumático**

U

ugly **feo**
umbrella **el paraguas**
uncle **el tío**
under ... **debajo de ...**
underground (railway)
    el metro
underpants **los calzoncillos**
understand **entender;**
    I don't understand
    no entiendo
underwear **la ropa interior**
United States
    Estados Unidos
university **la universidad**
unleaded **sin plomo**
until **hasta**
unusual **poco común**
up **arriba;** (upward)
    hacia arriba
urgent **urgente**
us: it's for us **es para
    nosotros/nosotras;**
    give it to us **dénoslo**
use **el uso;** (verb) **usar;** it's no
    use **no sirve de nada**
useful **útil**
usual **corriente**
usually **en general**

V

vacancies (rooms)
    habitaciones libres
vaccination **la vacuna**
vacuum cleaner **la aspiradora**
valley **el valle**
valve **la válvula**
vanilla **la vainilla**
vase **el jarrón**
veal **la** (carne de) **ternera**

vegetables **la verdura**
vegetarian **vegetariano**
vehicle **el vehículo**
very **muy;** *very much* **mucho**
vest **la camiseta**
vet **el veterinario**
video (tape) **la cinta
de vídeo;** (film) **el vídeo**
video games **los vídeo-juegos**
video recorder
el (aparato de) **vídeo**
view **la vista**
viewfinder **el visor de imagen**
villa **el chalet**
village **el pueblo**
vinegar **el vinagre**
violin **el violín**
visit **la visita; visitar** (verb)
visiting hours **las horas
de visita**
visitor **el/la visitante**
vitamin pills **las vitaminas**
vodka **el vodka**
voice **la voz**
voicemail **la mensajería
de voz**

W

wait **esperar;** *wait!* **¡espere!**
waiter **el camarero;** *waiter!*
¡camarero!
waiting room **la sala
de espera**
waitress **la camarera;**
waitress! **¡Oiga,** *por favor!*
Wales **Gales**
walk (stroll) **el paseo;** (verb)
andar; *to go for a walk*
ir de paseo
wall **la pared;** (outside)
el muro
wallet **la cartera**
want (verb) **querer**
war **la guerra**
wardrobe **el armario**
warm **caliente;** (weather)
caluroso
was **estaba/era**
washing machine **la zapatilla**
washing powder
**el jabón de lavadora,
el detergente**
washing-up liquid
el lavavajillas
wasp **la avispa**
watch **el reloj;** (verb) **mirar**
water **el agua**
waterfall **la cascada**
water heater
el calentador (de agua)

wave **la ola;** (verb) **agitar**
wavy (hair) **ondulado**
we **nosotros/nosotras**
weather **el tiempo**
website **la web site,
el sitio web**
wedding **la boda**
Wednesday **miércoles**
weeds **las malas hierbas**
week **la semana**
welcome (adj) **bienvenido;**
(verb) **dar la bienvenida;**
you're welcome
no hay de qué
wellington boots
las botas de agua
Welsh **galés/galesa**
were: you were (informal
singular) **eras/estabas;**
(formal singular) **era/
estaba;** (informal plural)
erais/estabais; (formal
plural) **eran/estaban;** *we
were* **éramos/
estábamos;** *they were*
eran/estaban
west **el oeste**
wet **mojado**
what? **¿qué?**
wheel **la rueda**
wheel brace
la llave de las tuercas
wheelchair **la silla de ruedas**
when? **¿cuándo?**
where? **¿dónde?**
whether **si**
which? **¿cuál?**
whisky **el whisky**
white **blanco**
white coffee
el café con leche
who? **¿quién?**
why? **¿por qué?**
wide **ancho;** *3 metres wide*
**de tres metros
de anchura**
wife **la mujer**
wind **el viento**
window **la ventana**
windscreen **el parabrisas**
wine **el vino**
wine list **la carta de vinos**
wine merchant **el vinatero**
wing **el ala**
with **con**
without **sin**
witness **el testigo**
woman **la mujer**
wood (material) **la madera**
wool **la lana**
word **la palabra**

work **el trabajo;** (verb)
trabajar; (to function)
funcionar
worktop **el mostrador**
worse **peor**
worst **(el) peor**
wrapping paper **el papel de
envolver;** (for presents)
el papel de regalo
wrench **la llave inglesa**
wrist **la muñeca**
writing paper **el papel
de escribir**
wrong **equivocado**

X, Y, Z

x-ray department
el servicio de radiología
year **el año**
yellow **amarillo**
yes **sí**
yesterday **ayer**
yet **todavía;** *not yet*
todavía no
yoghurt **el yogur**
you (informal singular)
tú; (formal singular)
usted; (informal plural,
m/f) **vosotros/ vosotras;**
(formal plural) **ustedes**
young **joven**
your: your book (informal
singular) **tu libro;** (formal
singular) **su libro;** *your
shoes* (informal singular)
tus zapatos; (formal
singular) **sus zapato**
yours: is this yours? (informal)
¿es tuyo esto?; (formal)
¿es suyo esto?
youth hostel
el albergue juvenil
zip **la cremallera**
zoo **el zoo**

DICTIONARY
Spanish to English

The gender of Spanish nouns listed here is indicated by the abbreviations (m) for masculine nouns and (f) for feminine nouns. Plural nouns are followed by the abbreviations (m pl) or (f pl). Spanish adjectives (adj) vary according to the gender and number of the word they describe, and the masculine form is shown here. In general, adjectives that end in **-o** adopt an **-a** ending in the feminine form, and those that end in **-e** usually stay the same. For the plural form, **-s** is added.

A

a *to*; **a América** *to America*; **a la estación** *to the station*; **al médico** *to the doctor*; **a las tres** *at 3 o'clock*

abanico (m) *fan (handheld)*

abierto *open* (adj)

abogado/abogada (m/f) *lawyer*

abrebotellas (m) *bottle opener*

abrelatas (m) *can opener*

abrigo (m) *coat*

abril *April*

abrir *to open*

abuela (f) *grandmother*

abuelo (m) *grandfather*

abuelos (m pl) *grandparents*

aburrido *boring*

acaba de llegar *it's just arrived*

accidente (m) *accident*

aceite (m) *oil*; **el aceite de oliva** *olive oil*

aceituna (f) *olive*

acelerador (m) *accelerator*

acera (f) *pavement*

acondicionador (m) *conditioner (hair)*

acuerdo: me acuerdo *I remember*; **no me acuerdo** *I don't remember*

adaptador (m) *adaptor*

adelantar *overtake (car)*

adiós *goodbye*

aduana (f) *customs*

aerodeslizador (m) *hovercraft*

aeropuerto (m) *airport*

afeitado (m) *shave*; **afeitarse** *to have a shave*

after-shave (m) *aftershave*

afueras (f pl) *suburbs*

agencia (f) *agency*

agencia de viajes (f) *travel agency*

agenda (f) *diary*

agitar *to wave*

agosto *August*

agradable *pleasant*

agradecer *to thank*

agua (m) *water*; **el agua con gas** *fizzy water*; **el agua mineral** *mineral water*; **el agua potable** *drinking water*; **el agua sin gas** *still water*

aguja (f) *needle*

ahora *now*; **¿y ahora qué?** *what next?*

aire (m) *air*

aire acondicionado (m) *air conditioning*

ajedrez (m) *chess*

ajo (m) *garlic*

ajustado *tight*

ala (m) *wing*

albañil (m) *builder*

albaricoque (m) *apricot*

albergue juvenil (m) *youth hostel*

alcachofa (f) *artichoke*

alcohol (m) *alcohol*

alegre *glad*

alemán *German*

Alemania *Germany*

alérgico *allergic*

alfiler (m) *pin*

alfombra (f) *carpet; rug*

algo *something*

algodón (m) *cotton, cotton wool*

alguien *somebody*

alguna: en alguna parte *somewhere*

allí *there, over there*

almohada (f) *pillow*

alojamiento (m) *accommodation*

alquilar *to hire*

alto *high, tall, loud*

¡alto! *stop!*

amante (m/f) *lover*

amargo *bitter*

amarillo *yellow*

ambulancia (f) *ambulance*

América *America*

americano/americana (m/f) *American*

amigo/amiga (m/f) *friend*; **amigo/amiga por correspondencia** (m/f) *pen pal*

amontillado *medium (sherry)*

amor (m) *love*

ampliación (f) *enlargement*

ampolla (f) *blister*

análisis de sangre (m) *blood test*

andar *to walk*

andén (m) *platform*

anfiteatro (m) *lecture theatre*

anfitriona (f) *hostess*

anillo (m) *ring (jewellery)*

animal (m) *animal*; **los animales de compañía/los animales domésticos** *pets*

año (m) *year*

antes de ... *before ...*

anticonceptivo (m) *contraceptive*

anticongelante (m) *antifreeze*

anticuario (m) *antique shop*

antiséptico (m) *antiseptic*

aparcamiento (m) *car park*

aparcar *to park*; **prohibido aparacar** *no parking*

apartamento (m) *apartment*

apellido (m) *surname*

aperitivo (m) *aperitif*

apetito (m) *appetite*

aprender *learn*

aprendiz (m) *trainee*
apretón de manos (m) *handshake*
araña (f) *spider*
árbol (m) *tree*
árbol de levas (m) *camshaft*
arcón (m) *chest* (furniture)
arena (f) *sand*
Argelia *Algeria*
armario (m) *cupboard, wardrobe*
arreglar *repair*
arriba *up;* **hacia arriba** *upward*
arroyo (m) *stream* (small river)
arroz (m) *rice*
arte (m) *art*
artículos de punto (m pl) *knitwear*
artista (m/f) *artist*
asado *roasted*
ascensor (m) *lift*
asiento (m) *seat;* **el asiento infantil** *car seat* (for a baby/child)
asistenta (f) *cleaner*
asmático *asthmatic*
aspiradora (f) *vacuum cleaner*
aspirina (f) *aspirin*
atar *to tie*
atasco (m) *traffic jam*
aterrizar *to land*
ático (m) *attic*
atractivo *attractive* (offer)
audífono (m) *hearing aid*
auriculares (m pl) *headphones*
Australia *Australia*
australiano/australiana (m/f) *Australian*
autobús (m) *bus;*
autobús del aeropuerto *airport bus*
autocaravana (f) *camper van*
automático *automatic*
autónomo/autónoma (m/f) *self-employed*
autopista (f) *motorway*
avería (f) (car) *breakdown;* **he tenido una avería** *I've had a breakdown*
aves (f pl) *poultry*
avión (m) *aircraft*
avispa (f) *wasp*
ayer *yesterday*
ayuda (f) *help*
ayudar *to help*
ayuntamiento (m) *town hall*
azúcar (m) *sugar*
azul *blue*

B

bacon (m) *bacon*
bailar *to dance*
baile (m) *dance*
bajarse *to get off* (bus etc) ; *to get out*
bajo *low, short*
balandro (m) *sailing boat*
balcón (m) *balcony*
Baleares: las (Islas) **Baleares** *Balearic Islands*
balón (m) *football* (ball); **el balón de playa** *beach ball*
baloncesto (m) *basketball*
bañador (m) *bathing suit, swimming trunks*
banco (m) *bank*
banda (f) *band* (musicians)
bandeja (f) *tray*
bandera (f) *flag*
baño (m) *bath, bathroom, toilet* (room in a house); **darse un baño** *to have a bath;* **el traje de baño** *bathing suit*
bar (m) *bar* (drinks)
baraja (f) *deck of cards*
barato *inexpensive*
barba (f) *beard*
barbacoa (f) *barbecue*
barca (f) *small boat;* **la barca de remos** *rowing boat*
barco (m) *boat, ship*
barra de labios (f) *lipstick*
bastante *enough, quite, fairly*
basura (f) *litter, rubbish*
batería (f) *battery* (car)
bebé (m) *baby*
beber *to drink;* **¿quiere beber algo?** *would you like something to drink?*
bebida (f) *drink*
beige *beige*
beneficios (m pl) *profits*
berenjenas (f pl) *aubergines*
biblioteca (f) *library*
bicicleta (f) *bicycle;* **la bicicleta de montaña** *mountain bike*
bien *good;* **te sienta bien** *it suits you*
bienvenido *welcome*
bigote (m) *moustache*
billete (m) *fare, ticket* (train etc); **billete de ida y vuelta** (m) *return ticket*

billete de banco (m) *banknote*
bizcocho (m) *sponge cake*
blanco *white*
blando *soft*
bloc (m) *notepad*
bloque de oficinas (m) *office block*
blusa (f) *blouse*
boca (f) *mouth*
bocadillo (m) *sandwich*
boda (f) *wedding*
bodega (f) *cellar*
bolígrafo (m) *ballpoint pen*
bollo (m) *roll* (bread)
bolsa (f) *bag, packet* (sweets, crisps); **la bolsa de basura** *bin liner;* **la bolsa de plástico** *plastic bag*
bolsillo (m) *pocket*
bolso (m) *handbag*
bombilla (f) *light bulb*
bonito *nice, pretty, attractive* (object)
bordado (m) *embroidery*
borde (m) *edge, border, side*
borracho *drunk*
bosque (m) *forest*
bota (f) *boot*
botas de agua (f pl) *wellington boots*
botella (f) *bottle*
botón (m) *button*
brazo (m) *arm*
bridge (m) *bridge* (game)
británico/británica (m/f) *British*
brocha (f) *paint brush*
broche (m) *brooch*
broma (f) *joke*
bronceado *suntanned*
broncearse *suntan: to get a suntan*
buenas noches *good evening*
buenas tardes *good afternoon*
bueno *good, good to eat, tasty*
buenos días *good morning*
bufanda (f) *scarf*
buzón (m) *postbox*

C

cabeza (f) *head*
cabina telefónica (f) *phone booth*
cable alargador (m) *extension cord*
cacahuetes (m pl) *peanuts*
cada *every, each;* **viente euros cada uno** *20 euros each*

café (m) *café, coffee;*
el café con leche
white coffee; **el café**
instantáneo *instant coffee;*
el café solo *espresso*
caja (f) *box; check-out;* **la caja**
de bombones *box of*
chocolates; **la caja de**
cambios *gearbox*
cajero (m) *cashier;*
el cajero automático
ATM, cashpoint
cajetilla (f) *packet* (cigarettes)
calambre (m) *cramp*
calcetines (m pl) *socks*
calculadora (f) *calculator*
calefacción (f) *heating;*
la calefacción central
central heating
calentador (de agua) (m)
water heater
calidad (f) *quality*
caliente *warm*
callado *quiet* (person)
calle (f) *street;* **la calle**
principal *main road*
caluroso *warm* (weather)
calzoncillos (m pl) *underpants*
cama (f) *bed*
cámara de fotos (f) *camera*
cámara neumática (f)
inner tube
camarera (f) *waitress*
camarero (m) *waiter;*
¡camarero! *waiter!*
cambiar *to change* (money)
cambiarse *to change* (clothes)
cambio (m) *change* (money);
exchange rate
camino (m) *path*
camión (m) *truck*
camisa (f) *shirt*
camiseta (f) *vest*
camisón (m) *nightgown*
campana (f) *bell* (church)
camping (m) *campsite*
camping-gas (m) *camping gas*
campo (m) *countryside, field*
Canadá *Canada*
canadiense *Canadian*
canal (m) *canal*
Canarias: las (Islas)
Canarias Canaries
canción (f) *song*
candado (m) *padlock*
cangrejo (m) *crab*
cansado *tired*
cantar *to sing*
capazo (m) *crib*
capó (m) *bonnet* (car)
cara (f) *face*

caramelos (m) *sweets*
caravana (f) *trailer*
carburador (m) *carburetor*
cardenal (m) *bruise*
cargador (m) *charger*
carne (f) *meat*
carne de cerdo (f) *pork*
carne de vaca (f) *beef*
carnet de conducir (m)
driving licence
carnicería (f) *butcher's*
caro *expensive*
carpintero (m) *carpenter*
carretera (f) *road*
carrito (m) *trolley*
carta (f) *letter* (mail); *menu;* **la**
carta de vinos (f) *wine list*
cartera (f) *purse, briefcase,*
wallet
carterista (m) *pickpocket*
cartero (m) *postman*
casa (f) *house, home;*
en casa *at home*
casado *married*
cascada (f) *waterfall*
casi *almost*
cassette (f) *cassette*
castaño *brown* (hair)
castañuelas (f pl) *castanets*
castellano *Castilian*
Castilla *Castile*
castillo (m) *castle*
Cataluña *Catalonia*
catedral (f) *cathedral*
catedrático (m) *professor*
católico *Catholic* (adj)
catorce *fourteen*
cazo (m) *saucepan*
cebo (m) *bait*
cebolla (f) *onion*
ceja (f) *eyebrow*
cementerio (m) *cemetery*
cena (f) *dinner, supper,*
dinner party
cenicero (m) *ashtray*
centro (m) *centre; city centre;*
el centro deportivo *sports*
centre; **en el centro**
middle: in the middle
cepillar el pelo *to brush hair*
cepillo (m) *brush* (for cleaning);
el cepillo del pelo *hair*
brush; **el cepillo de**
dientes *toothbrush*
cerca *near, close;* (f) *fence*
cereza (f) *cherry*
cerilla (f) *match* (light)
cerrado *closed*
cerrar *to close*
cerrojo (m) *bolt* (on door)
certificado (m) *certificate*

cerveza (f) *beer*
césped (m) *lawn*
cesto (m) *basket*
chal (m) *shawl*
chalet (m) *villa*
champiñones (m pl)
mushrooms
champú (m) *shampoo*
chandal (m) *track suit*
chaparrón (m) *shower* (rain)
chaqueta (f) *jacket*
charcutería (f) *delicatessen*
charla (f) *talk*
cheque (m) *cheque;*
el cheque de viaje
traveller's cheque
chica (f) *girl*
chicle (m) *chewing gum*
chico (m) *boy*
chimenea (f) *chimney,*
fireplace
chincheta (f) *drawing pin*
chiste (m) *joke* (funny story)
chocolate (m) *chocolate*
chuleta (f) *chop* (food)
chupa-chups (m) *lollipop*
ciclismo (m) *cycling*
ciclomotor (m) *moped*
ciego *blind* (cannot see)
cielo (m) *sky*
cien *hundred*
ciencias (f pl) *science*
cierto *true*
cigalas (f pl) *crayfish*
cigarrillo (m) *cigarette*
cinco *five*
cincuenta *fifty*
cine (m) *cinema*
cinta (f) *cassette;* **el cinta**
de vídeo *video tape*
cinturón (m) *belt;* **el cinturón**
de seguridad *seat belt*
cita (f) *appointment*
ciudad (f) *city, town;*
el centro ciudad *city centre*
claro *clear* (water); *light*
(adj: not dark)
clase (f) *class; lesson*
clavo (m) *nail* (metal)
claxon (m) *horn* (car)
cliente (m) *client*
cobrador (m) *conductor* (bus)
cobrar *to cash*
cocer *to cook, boil*
cocer al horno *to bake*
coche (m) *car*
coche-cama (m) *sleeper car*
cochecito (m) *pram*
cocina (f) *cooker; kitchen*
cocinero/cocinera (m/f) *cook*
coctel (m) *cocktail party*

código *code;* **el código de la circulación** *highway code;* **el código** *postal postcode*
codo (m) *elbow*
coger *catch;* **coger el tren** *to catch the train*
cojín (m) *cushion*
col (f) *cabbage*
cola (f) *line*
colada (f) *laundry (washed)*
colcha (f) *bedspread*
colchón (m) *mattress*
colchoneta (f) *air mattress*
colección (f) *collection (stamps etc)*
coliflor (f) *cauliflower*
collar (m) *collar (of animal)*
collar (m) *necklace; colour*
combinacíon (f) *slip (underwear)*
comedor (m) *dining room*
comer *to eat*
comida (f) *food, meal; lunch*
comida ligera (f) *snack*
comisaría (f) *police station*
como *like;* **como éste** *like this one*
¿cómo? *how?;* **¿cómo se llama usted?** *what's your name?;* **¿cómo dice?** *pardon?, what did you say?*
cómoda (f) *chest of drawers*
compañía aérea (f) *airline*
compartimento (m) *compartment*
completamente *completely*
complicado *complicated*
compra (f) *shopping*
comprar *to buy*
comprendo *I see*
compresas (f pl) *sanitary towels*
con *with*
coñac (m) *brandy*
concha (f) *shell*
concierto (m) *concert*
concurrido *crowded*
condón (m) *condom*
conducir *to drive*
conductor (m) *driver*
conejo (m) *rabbit*
conferencia (f) *conference;* **la sala de conferencias** *conference room*
congelador (m) *freezer*
congelados (m pl) *frozen foods*
conocer *to know (person, place)*
conserje (m) *porter (hotel)*
consulado (m) *consulate*
contable (m/f) *accountant*
contendor de basura (m) *bin*
contento *happy*

contestador automático (m) *answering machine*
contra *against*
contraseña (f) *password*
contrato (m) *contract*
copa (f) *glass (for drinking)*
corazón (m) *heart*
corazones (m pl) *hearts (cards)*
corbata (f) *tie*
corcho (m) *cork*
cordero (m) *lamb*
cordones (de los zapatos) (m pl) *(shoe)laces*
correa (f) *lead*
correcto *right (correct)*
correo (m) *mail, post;* **el correo certificado** *registered post;* **el correo electrónico** *email*
Correos: (la oficina de) **Correos** (f) *post office*
correr *to run*
corrida de toros (f) *bullfight*
corriente *ordinary; usual*
cortadura (f) *cut*
cortar *to chop, cut*
cortauñas (m pl) *nail clippers*
corte de pelo (m) *haircut*
cortina (f) *curtain*
corto *short*
coser *to sew*
cosméticos (m pl) *cosmetics*
costar *to cost;* **¿cuánto cuesta?** *what does it cost?*
crema (f) *cream (lotion)*
crema de zapatos (f) *shoe polish*
cremallera (f) *zip*
creo que ... *I think that ...*
crepes (f pl) *pancakes*
crisis nerviosa (f) *nervous breakdown*
cristal (m) *glass (material)*
crucero (m) *cruise*
cuaderno (m) *notebook*
cuadrado *square (adj)*
¿cuál? *which?*
cualquiera de ellos *either of them*
¿cuándo? *when?*
¿cuánto cuesta? *what does it cost?, how much is it?*
¿cuántos años tiene? *how old are you?*
cuarenta *forty*
cuarto (m) *quarter, room;* (adj) *fourth*
cuarto de baño (m) *bathroom*
cuarto de estar (m) *living room, lounge*
cuatro *four*

cubo (m) *bucket;* **el cubo de la basura** *dustbin*
cucaracha (f) *cockroach*
cuchara (f) *spoon*
cuchillas de afeitar (f pl) *razor blades*
cuchillo (m) *knife*
cuello (m) *neck, collar*
cuenco (m) *bowl*
cuenta (f) *bill*
cuerda (f) *string; rope*
cuerno (m) *horn (animal)*
cuero (m) *leather*
cuerpo (m) *body*
cueva (f) *cave*
¡cuidado! *be careful!*
cumpleaños (m) *birthday*
cuna (f) *cot*
cura (m) *priest*
curry (m) *curry*

D

dar *give;* **dar la bienvenida** *to welcome*
de *of;* **de algún** *modo somehow;* **de ida** *single (ticket)*
debajo de *below, under*
decir *say;* **¿qué ha dicho?** *what did you say?;* **¿cómo se dice ...?** *how do you say ...?*
declaración (f) *statement*
dedo (m) *finger*
delante de *in front of ...*
delgado *thin*
demasiado *too (excessively)*
démelo *give it to me*
dentadura postiza (f) *dentures, false teeth*
dentista (m/f) *dentist*
denuncia (f) *police report*
departamento (m) *department*
deporte (m) *sport*
derecho (m) *law, justice;* **no hay derecho** *it's not fair;* (adj) *right (not left)*
desayuno (m) *breakfast*
descansar *to rest*
descuento (m) *discount*
desmayarse *to faint*
desodorante (m) *deodorant*
despacho (m) *office (room)*
despegue (m) *take off*
despertador (m) *alarm clock*
después *then (after);* **después de** ... *after ...*
destornillador (m) *screwdriver*
detergente (m) *washing powder*
detrás de ... *behind ...*
devolver *to return (give back); to be sick (vomit)*

día (m) day; **el día de fiesta** public holiday
diabético diabetic
diamantes (m pl) diamonds
diarrea (f) diarrhoea
diccionario (m) dictionary
diciembre December
diecinueve nineteen
dieciocho eighteen
dieciséis sixteen
diecisiete seventeen
diente (m) tooth
diesel diesel (adj: engine)
diez ten
diferente different
difícil difficult
dígame hello (on phone)
dinero (m) money, cash; **no tengo dinero** I have no money
dirección (f) address
director/directora (m/f) manager (hotel); conductor (orchestra)
disco (m) record (music)
disco compacto (m) compact disc
discoteca (f) nightclub
diseñador/diseñadora (m/f) designer
disponible available
distancia distance; **¿qué distancia hay a ...?** how far is it to ...?
distinto separate, different (adj); **¡eso es distinto!** that's different!; **quería otro distinto** I'd like a different one
diversiones (f pl) entertainment
divertido; (odd) **raro** funny
divorciado divorced
doce twelve
documento (m) document
dólar (m) dollar
dolor (m) ache, pain; **el dolor de cabeza** headache; **el dolor de estómago** stomach-ache; **el dolor de muelas** toothache
domingo Sunday
¿dónde? where?; **¿dónde está ...?** where is ...?
dónut (m) doughnut
dormir to sleep
dormitorio (m) bedroom
dos two; **los dos** both
ducha (f) shower (bath)
dulce sweet (adj: not sour)
dunas (f pl) sand dunes
durante during
duro hard (not soft)
duty-free (m) duty-free shop

E

echar al correo to post
echar el cerrojo to bolt
edificio (m) building
edredón (m) duvet
eje (m) axle
ejecutivo (m) executive
ejemplo (m) example; **por ejemplo** for example
él he, him, the (m); **es para él** it's for him
elástico elastic
electricidad (f) electricity
electricista (m/f) electrician
eléctrico electric
ella she, her, the (f); **es para ella** it's for her
ellos/ellas they, them; **es para ellos/ellas** it's for them
email (m) email; **la dirección de email** email address
embajada (f) embassy
embarazada pregnant
embarazoso embarrassing
emergencia (f) emergency
empaste (m) filling (in tooth)
empezar to start
empleado (m) employee
empujar to push
en on, at, in; **en inglés** in English; **en el hotel** in the hotel; **en Barcelona** in Barcelona; **en Correos** at the post office; **en su casa** at your place
encaje (m) lace
encantado/encantada (m/f) pleased to meet you
encargado (m) caretaker
encendedor (m) lighter
encendido (m) ignition
enchufe (m) plug (electrical)
encima de ... over ...
encuentro (m) meeting; **no me encuentro bien** I don't feel well
enero January
enfermo/enferma (m/f) nurse
enfrente de opposite; **enfrente del hotel** opposite the hotel
¡enhorabuena! congratulations!
ensalada (f) salad

entender to understand; **no entiendo** I don't understand
entonces then, so
entrada (f) entrance, ticket (theatre etc)
entrantes (m pl) starters
entre ... between ...
entrega (f) delivery
enviar por fax to fax
epiléptico epileptic
equipaje (m) luggage; **el equipaje de mano** hand luggage
equipo de música (m) music system
equivocación (f) mistake
equivocado wrong
era you were (formal): it/he/she was
éramos we were
eran they were
eras you were (informal)
eres you are (informal)
es you are (formal)
es it/he/she is
escalera (f) staircase; **la escalera mecánica** escalator; **las escaleras** stairs
escarcha (f) frost
escocés/escocesa (m/f) Scottish
Escocia Scotland
escopeta (f) gun (rifle)
escuela (f) school
ese/esa that; **ese autobús** that bus; **ese hombre** that man; **esa mujer** that woman; **¿qué es eso?** what's that?
ése/ésa that, that one;
esmalte de uñas (m) nail polish
esos/esas those, those ones; **esos hombres** those men; **esas mujeres** those women
espalda (f) back (body)
España Spain
español/española (m/f) Spanish, Spaniard
especialidad (f) field of study
espejo (m) mirror
esperar to wait; **¡espere!** wait!
espinacas (f pl) spinach
espuma de afeitar (f) shaving foam
espuma moldeadora (f) mousse (for hair)
esquina (f) corner (of street)

esquís (m pl) *skis*
está *you are* (formal)
está *it/he/she is*
esta noche *tonight*
estaba *it/he/she was; you were* (formal)
estábamos *we were*
estaban *they were*
estabas *you were* (informal)
estaca (f) *tent peg*
estación (f) *station;* **la estación de autobuses** *bus station;* **la estación de esquí** *ski resort;* **la estación de metro** *metro station*
Estados Unidos *United States*
estamos *we are*
están *they are*
estanco (m) *tobacconist*
estaquilla (f) *tent peg*
estás *you are* (informal)
estatua (f) *statue*
este *east;* **el Este** *the East*
éste/ésta *this, this one;* **este hombre** *this man;* **esta mujer** *this woman;* **¿qué es esto?** *what's this?;* **éste es el señor ...** *this is Mr ...*
estómago (m) *stomach*
estos/estas *these, these ones;* **estos hombres** *these men;* **estas mujeres** *these women;* **éstos son míos** *these are mine*
estoy *I am*
estrecho *narrow* (adj)
estrella (f) *star*
estudiante (m/f) *student*
estufa (f) *heater*
estúpido *stupid*
etiqueta (f) *label*
evidente *clear* (obvious)
excelente *excellent*
exceso de equipaje (m) *excess baggage*
excursión (f) *excursion, tour*
exposición (f) *exhibition*
externa *external*
extintor (m) *fire extinguisher*
extranjero/extranjera (m/f) *foreigner*

F

fácil *easy*
factor de protección (m) *protection factor* (SPF)
factura (f) *invoice*
facturación (f) *check-in*
facturar *to check in*
falda (f) *skirt*
falta: no hace falta *there's no need*
familia (f) *family*
fan (m) *fan* (enthusiast)
fantástico *fantastic*
farmacia (f) *chemist*
faros (m pl) *headlights*
fax (m) *fax*
febrero *February*
¡felicidades! *happy birthday!*
feliz *happy*
feo *ugly*
feria (f) *fair, trade fair*
ferretería (f) *hardware store*
ferrocarril (m) *railway*
ferry (m) *ferry*
fiebre (f) *temperature,* **fever;** **la fiebre del heno** *hay fever*
fiesta (f) *party* (celebration)
filete (m) *steak*
filtro (m) *filter*
fin (m) *end;* **¡por fin!** *at last!*
final (m) *end*
fino *dry* (sherry)
flash (m) *flash* (camera)
flauta (f) *flute*
flequillo (m) *fringe* (hair)
flexo (m) *angle-poise lamp*
flor (f) *flower*
folleto (m) *brochure, leaflet*
fonda (f) *inn*
fondo (m) *bottom*
fontanero/fontanera (m/f) *plumber*
foto (grafía) (f) *photograph*
fotocopiadora (f) *photocopier*
fotografiar *to photograph*
fotógrafo (m) *photographer*
fotómetro (m) *light meter*
frambuesa (f) *raspberry*
francés *French*
Francia *France*
fregadero (m) *sink*
freír *to fry*
frenar *to brake*
freno (m) *brake;* **el freno de emergencia** *emergency brake;* **el freno de mano** *handbrake*
fresas (f pl) *strawberries*
fresco *cool*
frigorífico (m) *fridge*
frío cold (adj); *I'm cold* **tengo frío**
frito *fried*
frontera (f) *border* (between countries)
fruta (f) *fruit*

fuego (m) *fire;* **los fuegos artificiales** *fireworks*
fuel-oil *diesel* (oil)
fuente (f) *fountain*
fuera *outside*
fuerte *strong*
fumar *to smoke*
funcionar *to work* (function)
fútbol (m) *football* (game)

G

gabardina (f) *raincoat*
gafas (f pl) *glasses;* **las gafas de sol** *sunglasses*
galería de arte (f) *art gallery*
Gales *Wales*
galés/galesa *Welsh*
galleta (f) *biscuit*
gambas (f pl) *prawns*
ganga (f) *bargain*
garage (m) *garage* (for parking)
garantía (f) *guarantee*
garantizar *to guarantee*
garganta (f) *throat*
gas para el encendedor (m) *lighter fuel*
gasolina (f) *petrol*
gasolinera (f) *petrol station*
gato (m) *cat*
gay *gay* (homosexual)
gel (m) *gel* (hair); **el gel de ducha** *shower gel*
gemelos (m pl) *cuff links*
general: en general *usually*
gente (f) *people*
gerente (m/f) *manager*
Gibraltar *Gibraltar*
ginebra (f) *gin*
gobierno (m) *government*
Golfo de Vizcaya (m) *Bay of Biscay*
goma (f) *rubber band; rubber* (material)
goma de borrar (f) *eraser*
gordo *fat* (adj)
gorra (f) *cap* (hat)
gorro (m) *woollen hat*
gotas (f pl) *drops*
gracias *thank you*
Gran Bretaña *Great Britain*
grande *big, large*
grandes almacenes (m pl) *department store*
granja (f) *farm*
granjero (m) *farmer*
grapadora (f) *stapler*
grasa (f) *fat* (meat etc)
gratis *free* (no charge)
grifo (m) *tap*

gris grey
gritar to shout
grosellas negras (f pl) blackcurrants
grueso thick
grupo (m) party (group)
guantes (m pl) gloves
guapo attractive, beautiful, handsome (person)
guerra (f) war
guía (m/f) guide; **la guía telefónica** phone book; **la guía turística** guide book
guisantes (m pl) peas
guisar to cook
guitarra (f) guitar
gustar like: **me gusta ...** I like ...; **me gusta nadar** I like swimming

H

habitación (f) room; **la habitación doble** double room; **la habitación individual** single room; **habitaciones libres** vacancies
hablar to talk; **¿habla ...?** do you speak ...?; **no hablo ...** I don't speak ...
hacer to do, make; **hacer auto-stop** to hitchhike; **hacer footing** to jog; **hacer punto** to knit; **hacer transbordo** to change (trains etc); **hace sol** it's sunny
hacha (m) axe
hacia abajo down
hambre hungry; **tengo hambre** I'm hungry
hamburguesa (f) hamburger
hámster (m) hamster
harina (f) flour
hasta until
hay... there is/are...; **¿hay ...?** is/are there ...?
helado (m) ice cream
hepatitis (f) hepatitis
herida (f) injury
hermana (f) sister
hermano (m) brother
hervido boiled
hervidor de agua (m) kettle
hervir to boil (water)
hidroaleta (f) hydrofoil
hielo (m) ice
hierba (f) grass
hierro (m) iron (material)
hígado (m) liver

higo (m) fig
hija (f) daughter
hijastra (f) stepdaughter
hijastro (m) stepson
hijo (m) son
hincha (m) football fan
historia (f) history
hobby (m) hobby
hoguera (f) campfire
hoja (f) leaf, sheet (of paper)
hojalata (f) tin
hola hello
hombre (m) man
hombro (m) shoulder
homeopatía (f) homeopathy
honrado honest
hora (f) hour; **¿qué hora es?** what's the time?
horario (m) timetable; **el horario de apertura** opening times
horca (f) garden fork
horno (m) oven
horrible awful, horrible
hospital (m) hospital
hoy today
hueso (m) bone
huevo (m) egg
húmedo damp
humo (m) smoke

I

idioma (m) language
iglesia (f) church
imperdible (m) safety pin
imposible impossible
impreso de solicitud (m) application form
impresora (f) printer
incendio (m) fire (blaze)
incluido included
indigestión indigestion
infección (f) infection
información (f) information
informe (m) report
ingeniería (f) engineering
Inglaterra England
inglés/inglesa English
inhalador (m) inhaler (for asthma etc)
inmediatamente immediately
insecto (m) insect
insolación (f) sunstroke
insomnio (m) insomnia
instrumento musical (m) musical instrument
intentar to try
interesante interesting
intermitente (m) indicator

internet (m) internet
interpretar to interpret
intérprete (m/f) interpreter
interruptor (m) switch
intoxicación alimenticia (f) food poisoning
invitación (f) invitation
invitada (f) guest
inyección (f) injection
ir to go; **ir a esquiar** to go skiing; **ir de compras** to go shopping
Irlanda Ireland; **Irlanda del Norte** Northern Ireland
irlandés/irlandesa Irish
isla (f) island
Italia Italy
italiano/italiana (m/f) Italian
izquierdo left (not right)

J

jabón (m) soap; **el jabón de lavadora** washing powder
jamón (m) ham
jarabe (m) syrup
jardín (m) garden
jarrita (f) mug
jarrón (m) vase
jaula (f) cage
jazz (m) jazz
jefe (m) manager
jengibre (m) ginger (spice)
jerez (m) sherry
jeringuilla (f) syringe
jersey (m) sweater
joven young
joyería (f) jeweller's
judías (f pl) beans
jueves Thursday
jugar to play
juguete (m) toy
julio July
junio June
junto a near; **junto a la puerta** near the door; **junto a la ventana** near the window
juntos together

K, L

kilo (m) kilo
kilómetro (m) kilometre
kiosko de periódicos (m) newsagent's
la (f) the
laca (f) hairspray
lado de (f) beside
ladrón (m) thief

lago (m) *lake*
lámpara (f) *lamp*
lamparilla de noche (f) *bedside lamp*
lana (f) *wool*
langosta (f) *lobster*
lápiz (m) *pencil*
largo *long*
las (f pl) *the*
lata (f) *can* (tin)
lavabo (m) *basin* (sink)
lavandería automática (f) *laundrette*
lavavajillas (m) *dishwasher*
laxante (m) *laxative*
leche (f) *milk;* **la leche limpiadora** *cleansing milk* (for skin)
lechuga (f) *lettuce*
leer *to read*
lejía *bleach*
lejos *far, far away*
lengua (f) *tongue*
lente (f) *lens;* **las lentes de contacto** *contact lenses;* **las lentes de contacto semi-rígidas** *gas-permeable lenses*
lento *slow*
letra (f) *letter* (of alphabet)
levantarse *to get up* (rise)
libra (f) *pound* (sterling)
libre *free* (not engaged)
libre de impuestos *duty-free*
libro (m) *book;* **el libro de frases** *phrase book*
licor (m) *liqueur*
ligero *light* (adj: not heavy)
lima (f) *lime* (fruit)
lima de uñas (f) *nailfile*
límite de velocidad (m) *speed limit*
limón (m) *lemon*
limonada (f) *lemonade*
limpio *clean* (adj)
línea (f) *line* (phone etc)
linterna (f) *torch*
lista (f) *list*
listo *clever; ready*
literatura (f) *literature*
litro (m) *litre*
llamar por teléfono *to telephone*
llave (f) *key;* **la llave de las tuercas** *wheel brace;* **la llave inglesa** *wrench*
llegar *to arrive*
lleno *crowded, full;* **estoy lleno** *I'm full* (up)
llorar *to cry* (weep)
lluvia (f) *rain*

lo/la *it*
lo antes posible *as soon as possible*
loción *lotion* (f); **la loción anti-mosquitos** *insect repellent lotion;* **la loción bronceadora** *suntan lotion*
loco *mad*
lona impermeable (f) *groundsheet*
longitud (f) *length*
los (m pl) *the*
lo siento *I'm sorry*
luces de posición (f pl) *side lights*
lugar (m) *place, sight;* **los lugares de interés de ...** *the sights of ...*
luna (f) *moon*
lunes *Monday*
luz (f) *light*

M

madastra (f) *stepmother*
madera (f) *wood* (material)
madre (f) *mother*
maduro *ripe*
malas hierbas (f pl) *weeds*
maleta (f) *suitcase*
maletero (m) *boot* (car)
Mallorca *Majorca*
malo *bad, poor* (quality)
mama *Mum*
mañana *tomorrow*
mañana (f) *morning;* **por la mañana** *in the morning*
mandar *to send*
mandarina (f) *tangerine*
manga (f) *sleeve*
mano (f) *hand*
manta (f) *blanket, rug*
mantequilla (f) *butter*
manzana (f) *apple*
mapa (m) *map*
maquillaje (m) *make-up*
maquina cortacésped (f) *lawn mower*
máquina de escribir (f) *typewriter*
máquina de fotos (f) *camera*
mar (m) *sea*
marea (f) *tide*
mareado *faint, dizzy*
margarina (f) *margarine*
marido (m) *husband*
mariscos (m pl) *seafood, shellfish*
mármol (m) *marble*
marrón *brown*
Marruecos *Morocco*

martes *Tuesday*
martillo (m) *hammer*
marzo *March*
más *more;* **más de ...** *more than ...;* **más tarde** *later;* **algo más** *something else;* **alguien más** *someone else*
mástil (m) *tent pole*
matrícula (f) *number plate*
mayo *may*
mecánico (m) *mechanic*
media pensión *half board*
medianoche *midnight*
medias (f pl) *tights, stockings*
medicina (f) *medicine*
médico/médica (m/f) *doctor*
medio *half;* **media hora** *half an hour*
mediodía (m) *midday, noon*
Mediterráneo: el Mediterráneo *Mediterranean*
medusa (f) *jellyfish*
mejillones (m pl) *mussels*
mejor *best/better*
melocotón (m) *peach*
melón (m) *melon*
menos *less*
mensaje (m) *message*
mensajería de voz (f) *voicemail*
menú (del día) (m) *set menu*
menudo: a menudo *often*
mercado (m) *market*
mermelada (f) *jam;* **la mermelada de naranja** *marmalade*
mes (m) *month*
mesa (f) *table;* **la mesa de escritorio** *desk*
mesilla de noche (f) *bedside table*
metro (m) *underground* (railway)
mi (s) *my;* **mi libro** *my book;* **mis llaves** *my keys*
microondas (m) *microwave*
miel (f) *honey*
miércoles *Wednesday*
mil *thousand*
minusválido *disabled*
minuto (m) *minute*
mío *mine;* **es mío** *it's mine*
mirar *to watch*
misa (f) *mass* (church)
mismo *same;* **el mismo vestido** *the same dress;* **la misma gente** *the same people;* **lo mismo otra vez, por favor** *same again, please*

mochila (f) *backpack*
moda (f) *fashion*
modem (m) *modem*
mojado *wet*
moneda (f) *coin*
monedero (m) *purse*
monitor (m) *monitor*
montaña (f) *mountain*
monte (m) *hill*
monumento (m)
  monument
morado *purple*
moras (f pl) *blackberries*
mordedura (f) *bite (dog)*
morder *to bite (dog)*
morir *to die*
mosaico (m) *mosaic*
mosca (f) *fly (insect)*
mosquito (m) *mosquito*
mostaza (f) *mustard*
mostrador (m) *worktop*; **el
  mostrador de
  facturación** *check-in desk*
motocicleta (f) *motorcycle*
motor (m) *engine (motor)*
motora (f) *motorboat*
mover *to move (something)*;
  moverse *move oneself*; **¡no
  se mueva!** *don't move!*
mucho *much/many, a lot*;
  mucho mejor *much better*;
  mucho más despacio
  much slower; **no muchos**
  not many
mudarse *(de casa) to
  move (house)*
muebles (m pl) *furniture*
muela (f) *back tooth*
muelle (m) *dock*;
  spring (mechanical)
muerto *dead*
mujer (f) *woman, wife*
muletas (f pl) *crutches*
muñeca (f) *wrist*
muro (m) *wall (outside)*
museo (m) *museum*
música (f) *music*; **la música
  clásica** *classical music*;
  la música folklórica *folk
  music*; **la música pop** *pop
  music*
músico (m) *musician*
muy *very*

N

nací en ... *I was born in ...*
nada *nothing*; **no queda
  nada** *there's nothing left*; **no
  sirve de nada** *it's no use*
nadar *to swim*

nadie *nobody*
naranja (f) *orange (fruit)*;
  orange (adj)
nariz (f) *nose*
nata (f) *cream (dairy)*
natación (f) *swimming*
náuseas *sick*; **tengo náuseas**
  I feel sick
navaja (f) *penknife*
navidad (f) *Christmas*
necesario *necessary*
necesito ... *I need ...*
negar *to deny*
negativo (m) *negative
  (photo)*
negocio (m) *business*
negro *black*
**neozelandés/
  neozelandesa** *New
  Zealander*
neumático (m) *tyre*
ni ... ni ... *neither ... nor ...*
niebla (f) *fog*
nieta (f) *granddaughter*
nieto (m) *grandson*
nieve (f) *snow*
**ninguno/ninguna:
  ninguno de ellos** *neither
  of them*; **en ninguna
  parte** *nowhere*
niño/niña *child (m/f)*; **los
  niños** *children*;
  el niño pequeño *baby*
no *no (response), not*; **no hay
  de qué** *you're welcome*; **no
  importa** *it doesn't matter*;
  no es/está ... *(s) he's not ...*
noche (f) *night*
nombre (m) *name*; **el
  nombre de pila** *first name*
norte (m) *north*
nosotros/nosotras *we, us*; **es
  para nosotros/ nosotras**
  it's for us
noticias (f pl) *news*
novela (f) *novel*
noventa *ninety*
novia (f) *girlfriend*
noviembre *November*
novio (m) *boyfriend*
nudista (m/f) *nudist*
nuestro *our*; **es nuestro**
  it's ours
Nueva Zelanda
  New Zealand
nueve *nine*
nuevo *new*
nuez (f) *nut (fruit)*
número (m) *number*; **los
  números** *figures*
nunca *never*

O

o *or*; **o bien ... o ...** *either ...
  or ...*
obra de teatro (f)
  play (theatre)
obturador (m) *shutter
  (camera)*
Océano Atlántico (m)
  Atlantic Ocean
ochenta *eighty*
ocho *eight*
octubre *October*
oculista (m/f) *optician*
ocupado *busy (engaged)*;
  occupied
oeste (m) *west*
oficina (f) *office (place)*;
  branch (of company); **la
  oficina de objetos
  perdidos** *lost property
  office*; **la oficina de
  turismo** *tourist office*
oído (m) *(inner) ear*
¡oiga, por favor!
  excuse me! (to get attention);
  waiter/waitress!
oír *to hear*
ojo (m) *eye*
ola (f) *wave*
oler *to smell*
olivo (m) *olive tree*
olor (m) *smell*
oloroso *sweet (sherry)*
olvidar *to forget*
once *eleven*
ondulado *wavy (hair)*
operación (f) *operation*
operadora (f) *operator*
oporto (m) *port (drink)*
orden del día (m) *agenda*
ordenador (m) *computer*
oreja *ear* (f)
órgano (m) *organ (music)*
oro (m) *gold*
orquesta (f) *orchestra*
oscuro *dark*; **azul oscuro**
  dark blue
ostra (f) *oyster*
otra vez *again*
otro *another; other*;
  el otro *the other one*; **en
  otro sitio** *somewhere else*

P

padastro (m) *stepfather*
padre (m) *father*; **los padres**
  parents
pagar *to pay*; **pagar al
  contado** *to pay cash*

página (f) *page*
pago (m) *payment*
país (m) *country* (state)
pájaro (m) *bird*
pala (f) *spade*
palabra (f) *word*
palacio (m) *palace*
palanca de velocidades (f) *gear stick*
pálido *pale*
pan (m) *bread*
panadería (f) *bakery*
pañal (m) *nappy*; **los pañales desechables** *disposable nappies*
paño de cocina (m) *dish cloth*
pantalla (f) *lampshade, screen*
pantalón (m) *trousers*; **los pantalones cortos** *shorts*
pantis (m pl) *tights*
pañuelo (m) *headscarf*; **los pañuelos de papel** *tissues*
papá *dad*
papel (m) *paper*; **el papel de envolver/regalo** *wrapping paper*; **el papel de escribir** *writing paper*; **el papel higiénico** *toilet paper*; **los papeles de filtro** *filter papers*
paquete (m) *package, packet, parcel*
par (m) *pair*
para *for*; **es para mí** *it's for me*; **para el viernes** *by Friday*; **¿para qué?** *what for?*; **para una semana** *for a week*
parabrisas (m) *windscreen*
parachoques (m) *bumper*
parada (f) *stop* (bus); **la parada de taxis** *taxi rank*
parafina (f) *paraffin*
paraguas (m) *umbrella*
parar *to stop*
pared (f) *wall* (inside)
pariente (m) *relative*
parque (m) *park*
parrilla (f) *grill*
parte de atrás (f) *back* (not front)
parterre (m) *flowerbed*
partido (m) *match* (sport); *party* (political)
pasajero (m) *passenger*
pasaporte (m) *passport*; **el pasaporte de animales** *pet passport*
pasas (f pl) *raisins*
paseo (m) *walk, stroll*; **ir de**

paseo *to go for a walk*
pasillo (m) *aisle, corridor*
paso elevado (m) *flyover*
pasta (f) *pasta*
pasta dentífrica (f) *toothpaste*
pastel (m) *cake* (small)
pastelería (f) *cake shop*
pastilla (f) *pill, tablet*; **las pastillas de menta** *peppermints*; **las pastillas para la garganta** *cough drops*
patata (f) *potato*; **las patatas fritas** *chips, crisps*
patinar *to skid*
patines para hielo (m pl) *ice skates*
peatón (m) *pedestrian*
pecho (m) *chest* (part of body)
pedazo (m) *piece*
pedido (m) *order*
pegamento (m) *adhesive, glue*
peinar *to comb*
peine (m) *comb*
película (f) *film, movie*; **la película en color** *colour film*
peligroso *dangerous*
pelo (m) *hair*
pelota (f) *ball*
peluquería (f) *hairdresser*; **la peluquería de caballeros** *barber*
pendientes (m pl) *earrings*
pensar *to think*; **lo pensaré** *I'll think about it*
pensión completa *full board*
peor *worse, worst*
pepino (m) *cucumber*
pequeño *little, small*
pera (f) *pear*
percha (f) *coat hanger*
¡perdón! *sorry!, excuse me!* (when sneezing etc)
perejil (m) *parsley*
perezoso *lazy*
perfecto *perfect*
perfume (m) *perfume*
periódico (m) *newspaper*
perla (f) *pearl*
permanente (f) *perm*
permiso (m) *licence*
pero *but*
perro (m) *dog*
persianas (f pl) *blinds*
pesado *heavy*
pesca (f) *fishing*
pescadería (f) *fishmonger's*
pescado (m) *fish* (food)
pescar: ir a pescar *to go fishing*

pez (m) *fish* (animal)
piano (m) *piano*
picadura (f) *bite* (by insect)
picaporte (m) *handle* (door)
picar *to bite* (insect)
picas (f pl) *spades* (cards)
picnic (m) *picnic*
pie (m) *foot*
pierna (f) *leg*
pijama (m) *pyjamas*
pila (f) *battery* (torch etc)
piloto (m) *pilot*
pimienta (f) *pepper* (spice)
pimiento (m) *pepper* (red, green)
pin (m) *PIN*
piña (f) *pineapple*
pinchazo (m) *puncture*
pino (m) *pine* (tree)
pintor (m) *decorator*
pintura (f) *paint*
pinza (f) *peg*; **las pinzas** *tweezers*
pipa (f) *pipe* (for smoking)
Pirineos: los Pirineos *Pyrenees*
piscina (f) *swimming pool*; **la piscina municipal** *public swimming pool*
piso (m) *apartment*; *floor* (storey)
pista (f) *runway*
pistola (f) *gun* (pistol)
piston (m) *piston*
pizza (f) *pizza*
plancha (f) *iron* (for clothes); **a la plancha** *grilled*
planchar *to iron*
plano (m) *town map, town plan*; (adj) *flat, level*
planta (f) *plant*
planta baja (f) *ground floor*
plástico (m) *plastic*; **el plástico para envolver** *plastic wrap*
plata (f) *silver* (metal)
plátano (m) *banana*
plateado *silver* (colour)
platillo (m) *saucer*
plato (m) *plate*; **el plato principal** *main course*; **los platos preparados** *ready meals*
playa (f) *beach*
plaza (f) *pitch, square* (in town); **la plaza de toros** *bullring*
pluma (f) *pen*; **la pluma estilográfica** *fountain pen*
pobre *poor* (not rich)

poco *a little;* **poco común**
unusual; **poco hecho/**
pasado *rare (steak)*
poder *to be able*
policía (f) *police*
policía (m) *police officer*
política (f) *politics*
pollo (m) *chicken*
polvo (m) *powder;* **los polvos**
make-up powder; **los polvos**
de talco *talcum powder*
pomada (f) *ointment*
poner *to put;* **¿me pone ...?**
can I have ...?
poquito *a little;* **sólo**
un poquito *just a little*
por *through, by, per;* **por**
avión *by air mail;* **por la**
noche *at night;* **por la noche**
per night; **por todas** *partes*
everywhere
porcelana (f) *china (wear)*
por favor *please*
¿por qué? *why?*
porque *because*
portero (m) *caretaker*
Portugal *Portugal*
portugués *Portuguese*
posible *possible*
postal (f) *postcard*
póster (m) *poster*
postigo (m) *shutter (window)*
postre (m) *dessert*
precio (m) *price;* **el precio**
de entrada (m) *admission*
charge
precioso *beautiful (object)*
preferir *to prefer*
pregunta (f) *question*
presupuesto (m) *budget,*
estimate
primavera (f) *spring (season)*
primer piso (m) *first floor*
primero *first;* **de primera**
first class; **primeros**
auxilios *first aid*
primo (m) *cousin*
prima (f) *cousin*
principiante (m/f) *beginner*
principio (m) *start, beginning*
prisa: tengo prisa
I'm in a hurry
privado *private*
problema (m) *problem*
producto (m) *product;* **los**
productos de belleza
beauty products; **los**
productos del hogar
household products; **los**
productos lácteos *dairy*
products

profesión (f) *profession*
profesor/profesora (m/f)
teacher
profesor/profesora de
universidad (m/f) *lecturer*
(university)
profundo *deep*
programa (m) *schedule*
prohibido *prohibited*
prometida (f) *fiancée*
prometido (m) *fiancé*
prometido/prometida (m/f)
engaged (to be married)
propina (f) *tip (money)*
próximo *next*
prudente *careful*
prueba (f) *test*
público *public*
pueblo (m) *small town, village*
¿puede ...? *can you ...?*
puedo *I can;* **no puedo** *I can't*
puente (m) *bridge*
puerta (f) *door, gate;*
la puerta de embarque
departure gate
puerto (m) *harbour, port*
pulga (f) *flea*
pulpo (m) *octopus*
pulsera (f) *bracelet*
punta (f) *tip (end)*
puro (m) *cigar*

Q

que *than*
¿qué? *what?*
quemadura (f) *burn*
quemadura de sol (f)
sunburn
quemar *to burn*
querer *to want, love*
querido *dear (person)*
queso (m) *cheese*
¿qué tal? *how are you?*
¿quién? *who?*
quinze *fifteen*
quirófano (m) *operating*
theatre
quisquillas (f pl) *shrimps*
quizás *maybe, perhaps*

R

rábano (m) *radish*
radiador (m) *radiator*
radio (f) *radio*
rápido *fast, quick*
raro *rare (uncommon)*
rastrillo (m) *rake*
rata (f) *rat*
ratón (m) *mouse*

raya (f) *parting (hair)*
rebajas (f pl) *sale (at reduced*
prices)
rebeca (f) *cardigan*
recado (m) *message*
recepción (f) *reception*
recepcionista (m/f)
receptionist
receta (f) *prescription*
recibo (m) *receipt*
recobrar algo *to get*
something back
recogida (f) *collection (postal)*
récord (m) *record (sport etc)*
recuerdo (m) *souvenir*
redondo *round (circular)*
regalo (m) *gift;* **el regalo de**
cumpleaños *birthday*
present
regla (f) *ruler (for*
measuring)
reír *to laugh*
rejilla de equipajes (f)
luggage rack
relajarse *to relax*
religión (f) *religion*
relleno (m) *filling (in*
sandwich, cake)
reloj (m) *clock, watch*
remar *to row*
remolque (m) *trailer*
remos (m pl) *oars*
resaca (f) *hangover*
reserva (f) *reservation*
reservar *to book*
resfriado (m) *cold (illness);*
tengo un resfriado *I have*
a cold
respirar *to breathe*
restaurante (m) *restaurant*
resto (m) *rest, remainder*
retrasado *delayed;* **el**
autobús se ha retrasado
the bus is late
reunión (f) *meeting*
revelar *to develop (film)*
revista (f) *magazine*
rico *rich*
rímel (m) *mascara*
rincón (m) *corner (of room)*
riñón (m) *kidney*
río (m) *river*
rizos (m pl) *curls*
robar *steal;* **lo han robado**
it's been stolen
robo (m) *robbery*
roca (f) *rock (stone)*
rock (m) *rock (music)*
rodilla (f) *knee*
rojo *red*
ron (m) *rum*

ropa (f) *clothes;* **la ropa de cama** (f) *bed linen;* **la ropa interior** *underwear;* **la ropa sucia** *laundry* (dirty)
rosa (adj) *pink*
rosa (f) *rose*
roto *broken*
rotonda (f) *roundabout*
rotulador (m) *felt-tip pen*
roulotte (f) *caravan*
rubí (m) *ruby* (stone)
rubio *blond(e)* (adj)
rueda (f) *wheel;* **la rueda pinchada** *flat tyre*
rugby (m) *rugby*
ruidoso *noisy*
ruinas (f pl) *ruins*
rulos (m pl) *curlers*

S

sábado *Saturday*
sábana (f) *sheet* (bedding)
saber *to know* (fact); **no sé** *I don't know*
sabor (m) *flavour*
sacacorchos (m) *corkscrew*
sacapuntas (m) *pencil sharpener*
sacar *to bring out*
saco de dormir (m) *sleeping bag*
sal (f) *salt*
sala de espera (f) *waiting room*
sala de pediatría (f) *children's ward*
salchicha (f) *sausage*
salida (f) *exit, departure;* **las salidas** *departures;* **la salida de emergencia** *emergency exit*
salmón (m) *salmon*
salón (m) *lounge* (in hotel)
salsa (f) *sauce*
¡salud! *cheers!* (toast)
sandalias (f pl) *sandals*
sangre (f) *blood*
sartén (f) *frying pan*
sauna (f) *sauna*
secador (de pelo) (m) *hairdryer*
seco *dry*
sed *thirsty;* **tengo sed** *I'm thirsty*
seda (f) *silk*
segundo (m) *second* (noun; adj); **de segunda** *second class*
seguro (m) *insurance;* (adj) *sure, safe* (not dangerous)
seis *six*

sello (m) *stamp*
selva *rainforest*
semáforo (m) *traffic lights*
semana (f) *week;* **la semana pasada** *last week;* **la semana que viene** *next week*
seminario (m) *seminar*
semi-seco *medium-dry* (wine)
señal (f) *deposit*
sencillo *simple*
senderismo (m) *hiking*
señor *Mr, sir*
señora *Mrs, madam*
señorita *Miss*
separado *separated*
septiembre *September*
ser *to be*
serio *serious*
seropositivo *HIV positive*
servicio (m) *service, department;* **el servicio de habitaciones** *room service;* **el servicio de radiología** *x-ray department;* **el servicio de urgencias** *emergency department*
servicios (m pl) *toilets* (in public establishment); **los servicios de caballeros** *men's toilets;* **los servicios de señoras** *women's toilets*
servilleta (f) *napkin*
sesenta *sixty*
setas (f pl) *mushrooms*
setenta *seventy*
seto (m) *hedge*
si *if, whether*
sí *yes*
Sida (m) *AIDS*
siempre *always*
siete *seven*
significar: ¿qué significa esto? *what does this mean?*
siguiente *next*
silla (f) *chair;* **la silla de ruedas** *wheelchair*
sillita de ruedas (f) *stroller, pushchair*
simpático *friendly*
sin *without;* **sin plomo** *unleaded*
sinagoga (f) *synagogue*
sitio (m) *room, space;* **el sitio web** *website*
sobre (m) *envelope*
sobre todo *especially*
sobrina (f) *niece*
sobrino (m) *nephew*
soda (f) *soda water*

sofa (m) *sofa*
sofocante *close, stuffy*
sol (m) *sun*
solo *alone;* **yo solo** *by myself*
sólo *just, only*
soltero/soltera (m/f) *single* (unmarried)
solución limpiadora (f) *soaking solution* (for contact lenses)
sombrero (m) *hat*
sombrilla (f) *sunshade*
somnífero (m) *sleeping pill*
somos *we are*
son *they are*
sonreír *to smile*
sonrisa (f) *smile*
sopa (f) *soup*
sordo *deaf*
sostén (m) *bra*
sótano (m) *basement*
soy *I am;* **soy de …** *I come from …*
spray (m) *inhaler* (for asthma etc); **el spray antipulgas** *flea spray*
su (s) *its/hers/his/your* (formal); **¿es suyo esto?** *is this yours?*
subirse *to get in, get on* (of train, bus etc)
sucio *dirty*
sudadera (f) *sweatshirt*
Sudamérica *South America*
sudar *to sweat*
sudor (m) *sweat*
suelo (m) *floor;* **el suelo aislante** *groundsheet*
sueño (m) *sleep*
suerte (f) *luck;* **¡suerte!** *good luck!*
supermercado (m) *supermarket*
suplemento (m) *supplement*
supositorio (m) *suppository*
sur (m) *south*

T

tabaco (m) *tobacco*
tabla de windsurfing (f) *sailboard*
tableta de chocolate (f) *bar of chocolate*
tacón (m) *heel* (shoe)
taller (m) *garage* (for repairs)
talón (m) *heel* (foot)
talonario de cheques (m) *chequebook*
también *too* (also)
tampones (m pl) *tampons*

tan *so;* **tan bueno** *so good*
tanto: no tanto *not so much;*
  tanto ... como ... *both ...*
  and ...
tapiz (m) *tapestry*
tapón (m) *cap* (bottle),
  plug (sink)
taquilla (f) *box office,*
  ticket office
tarde (f) *evening;* (adj) *late; it's*
  getting late **se está**
  haciendo tarde
tarifa (f) *fare*
tarjeta (f) *card;* **la tarjeta de**
  banco *bank card;* **la tarjeta**
  de crédito *credit card;* **la**
  tarjeta de embarque
  boarding pass; **la tarjeta de**
  vista *business card;* **la**
  tarjeta telefónica
  phonecard
tarta (f) *cake* (large)
taxi (m) *taxi*
taza (f) *cup*
té (m) *tea*
techo (m) *ceiling*
teclado (m) *keyboard*
técnico (m) *technician*
tejado (m) *roof*
tejanos (m pl) *jeans*
tela (f) *material* (cloth)
teleférico (m) *cable car*
teléfono (m) *telephone; el*
  teléfono móvil *mobile phone*
televisión (f) *television;* **la**
  television por *cable cable*
  TV
temperatura (f) *temperature*
temprano *early*
tenedor (m) *fork*
tener *to have;* **tengo** *I have;*
  no tengo *I don't have;*
  ¿tiene? *do you have?;* **tengo**
  que irme *I have to go;*
  tengo calor *I feel hot;*
  tengo que ... *I must ...*
teñir *to bleach* (hair)
tenis (m) *tennis*
tenue *faint* (unclear)
tercero *third*
terminal (f) *terminal*
ternera (f) *veal*
terraza (f) *terrace*
testigo (m) *witness*
tía (f) *aunt*
tiempo (m) *time, weather*
tienda (f) *shop;* **la tienda de**
  comestibles grocer's; **la**
  tienda de discos *record*
  store
tienda (de campaña) (f) *tent*

¿tiene ...? *do you have ...?*
tierra (f) *land, soil*
tijeras (f pl) *scissors*
timbre (m) *bell* (door)
tinta (f) *ink*
tinto *red* (wine)
tintorería (f) *dry cleaner*
tío (m) *uncle*
tirantes (m pl) *braces*
tirar de *to pull*
tirita (f) *plaster*
toalla (f) *towel*
toallitas para bebé
  (f pl) *baby wipes*
tobillo (m) *ankle*
toca: me toca a mí
  it's my turn
tocadiscos (m) *record*
  player
tocar *to feel* (touch)
todavía *yet;* **todavía**
  no *not yet*
todo *everything, all;* **eso es**
  todo *that's all*
todos *everyone*
todos los días *every day*
tomar *to take;* **tomar el sol**
  to sunbathe
tomate (m) *tomato*
tónica (f) *tonic*
torero (m) *bullfighter*
tormenta (f) *storm*
tornillo (m) *screw*
toro (m) *bull*
torre (f) *tower*
tortilla (f) *omelette*
tos (f) *cough*
toser *to cough*
tostada (f) *toast*
trabajar *to work* (job)
trabajo (m) *job, work*
tractor (m) *tractor*
tradición (f) *tradition*
traducir *to translate*
traductor/traductora (m/f)
  translator
traer *to fetch*
tráfico (m) *traffic*
traje (m) *suit* (clothing)
tranquilo *quiet*
trapo del polvo (m) *duster*
trasero (m) *bottom*
  (part of body)
tréboles (m pl) *clubs*
  (cards)
trece *thirteen*
treinta *thirty*
tren (m) *train*
tres *three*
triste *sad*
tú *you* (informal)

tu (s) *your* (informal); **tu libro**
  your book; **tus zapatos** *your*
  shoes; **¿es tuyo esto?**
  is this yours?
tubería (f) *pipe* (for water)
tubo de escape (m) *exhaust*
tuerca (f) *nut* (for bolt)
tuerza (a la izquierda/
  derecha) *turn* (left/right)
túnel (m) *tunnel*
turismo (m) *sightseeing*
turista (m/f) *tourist*

U

último *last* (final)
ultramarinos (m) *grocer*
un/una *a*
uña (f) *finger nail*
único *single* (only)
universidad (f)
  university
uno *one*
urgente *urgent*
usar *to use*
uso (m) *use*
usted *you* (formal)
utensilios de cocina
  (m pl) *cooking utensils*
útil *useful*
uvas (f pl) *grapes*

V

vacaciones (f pl) *holiday*
vacío *empty*
vacuna (f) *vaccination*
vagón (m) *carriage* (train);
  el vagón-restaurante
  restaurant car
vainilla (f) *vanilla*
vale *OK*
valle (m) *valley*
válvula (f) *valve*
vapor (m) *steam, steamer*
  (boat); **al vapor**
  steamed
vaqueros (m pl) *jeans*
varios *several*
vaso (m) *glass* (for drinking)
váter (m) *toilet* (item in
bathroom)
¡váyase! *go away!*
veces: a veces
  sometimes
vegetariano *vegetarian*
vehículo (m) *vehicle*
veinte *twenty*
vela (f) *sailing; candle*
velocidad (f) *speed*
venda (f) *bandage*

vender to sell
veneno (m) poison
venir to vome; **¡venga aquí!** come here!
ventana (f) window
ventas (f pl) sales
ventilador (m) fan (ventilator)
ventisca (f) blizzard
ver to see; **no veo** I can't see
verdad true; **es verdad** it's true; **¿verdad?** isn't that so?
verde green
verdulería (f) greengrocer's
verdura (f) vegetables
verja (f) gate
vestido (m) dress
veterinario (m) vet
vez: de vez en cuando occasionally
viajar to travel; **viajar en avión** fly (of person)
viaje (m) journey; **el viaje de novios** honeymoon
vida (f) life
vídeo (m) video (film); **el (aparato de) vídeo** video recorder
videocámara (f) camcorder
vídeo-juegos (m pl) computer/video games
viejo old
viento (m) wind
viernes Friday
vigilante nocturno (m) night porter
vinagre (m) vinegar
vinatero (m) wine merchant
vino (m) wine
violín (m) violin
visita (f) visit; **las horas de visita** visiting hours; **la visita con guía** guided tour
visitante (m/f) visitor
visitar to visit
visor de imagen (m) viewfinder
vista (f) view
vitaminas (f pl) vitamin pills
vivero (m) garden centre
vodka (m) vodka
volar to fly (plane, insect)
volver to come/get back, return; **nos volvemos mañana** we get back tomorrow
voz (f) voice
vuelo (m) flight

W, Y, Z

web site (f) website
whisky (m) whisky
y and
ya already
yo I
yogur (m) yoghurt
zanahoria (f) carrot
zapatería (f) shoe shop
zapatilla (f) washing machine
zapatillas (f pl) slippers
zapatos (m pl) shoes; **los zapatos de deporte** trainers
zona peatonal (f) pedestrian zone
zoo (m) zoo
zumo juice (m); **el zumo de frutas** fruit juice; **el zumo de naranja** orange juice; **el zumo de tomate** tomato juice

Acknowledgments

The publisher would like to thank the following for their help: Isa Palacios and Maria Serna for the organization of location photography in Spain; Restaurant Raymon at Mi Pueblo, Madrid; Magnet Showroom, Enfield, London; MyHotel, London; Peppermint Green Hairdressers, London; Coolhurst Tennis Club, London; Kathy Gammon; Juliette Meeus and Harry.

Language content for Dorling Kindersley by G-and-W publishing.
Managed by **Jane Wightwick**; editing: **Cathy Gaulter-Carter, Teresa Cervera, Leila Gaafar**
Additional design assistance: **Phil Gamble, Lee Riches, Fehmi Cömert, Sally Geeve**
Additional editorial assistance: **Kajal Mistry, Paul Docherty, Lynn Bresler**
Picture research: **Louise Thomas**

Picture credits

Key: t=top; b=bottom; l=left; r=right; c=centre; A=above; B=below

p2 **DK Images**: *Joan Farre; p4/5* **Alamy RF**: *Image Source tl;* **Alamy**:*D Hurst bl; Indiapicture bcl; p10/11* **Alamy RF**: *BananaStock cAr;* **Getty**: *Taxi / James Day cBl;* **Ingram Image Library**: *bl; p12/13* **Alamy RF**: *Dynamics Graphics Group / Creatas cBr; John Foxx cAr; RubberBall br;* **DK Images**: *cl;* **Ingram Image Library**: *tl, cr; p14/15* **DK Images**: *tcr;* **Ingram Image Library**: *cl, cBl, cAr, cBr, bcr; p16/17* **Getty**: *Taxi / James Day bcr;* **Ingram Image Library**: *tr; p18/19* **DK Images**: *David Murray tr; p22/23* **DK Images**: *cl, Andy Crawford cAr; Susanna Price br; Magnus Rew tcrB;* **Ingram Image Library**: *tcr; p24/25* **DK Images**: *clA, Dave King tcr; p26/27* **Alamy RF**: *Dynamic Graphics Group / Creatas cl; p28/29* **DK Images**: *John Bulmer tcr; Dave King cr; Matthew Ward bclA;* **Ingram Image Library**: *bcrA, bcr; p30/31* **Alamy RF**: *Comstock Images bcl Think Stock bclA;* **DK Images**: *cl; p34/35* **Ingram Image Library**: *tcr; p36/37* **DK Images**: *bcl, bcr; Magnus Rew cl;* **Ingram Image Library**: *bl; p38/39* **Alamy RF**: *Imageshop / Zefa Visual Media cl;* **Ingram Image Library**: *cr; p40/41* **DK Images**: *Peter Wilson bl;* **Lee Riches**: *cl; p42/43* **Alamy RF**: *Image Source tcr, cAr, cAAr; p44/45* **Alamy**: *Jon Arnold Images br; ImageState / Ethel Davies bl; Vikki Martin cbl; Peter Titmuss bcrr;* **Alamy RF**: *Iain Davidson Photographic bcll; David O'Shea bcr; Courtesy of Renault: c; p46/47* **Alamy RF**: *Imageshop / Zefa Visual Media br;* **Ingram Image Library**: *cr; Courtesy of Renault: tcrB;* **Lee Riches**: *bcl; p48/49* **Alamy**: *Balearic Pictures c;* **Alamy RF**: *Brand X Pictures bcl;* **DK Images**: *tcr, bcl; Neil Lukas bcr; John Miller crA;* **Lee Riches**: *cl; p50/51* **Alamy**: *Peter Titmuss cr;* **Lee Riches**: *c; p52/53* **Alamy**: *Jean Dominique Dallet tcr;* **Alamy RF**: *Image Farm Inc cAr; Imageshop - Zefa Visual Media tcrB;* **DK Images**: *cl; Jackson Smith cBl;* **Alamy RF**: *Brand X Pictures cl; John Foxx c; Image Source cAr; ThinkStock tcr;* **DK Images**: *Andy Crawford bcl; p56/57* **Alamy**: *Balearic Pictures clA;* **Alamy RF**: *Brand X Pictures clAA;* **DK Images**: *cl; Neil Lukas tl; John Miller tcll;* **Lee Riches**: *tcl; Courtesy of Renault: bc; p58/59* **Alamy**: *Michael Juno tcr;* **Alamy RF**: *Brand X Pictures cBl, cBBl; Ingram Publishing cAAl;* **DK Images**: *cAl; Max Alexander cBr; p60/61* **Alamy**: *Robert Harding Picture Library bcr;* **Alamy RF**: *Image Source cAr;* **DK Images**: *Steve Gorton bl, tcrB; Pia Tryde cAAr;* **Ingram Image Library**: *cr; p62/63* **DK Images**: *Stephen Whitehorn c; p64/65* **Alamy**: *Arcaid bcrA; Mike Kipling c;* **Alamy RF**: *GKPhotography cBr; Goodshoot cAAr; Justin Kase tcrB;* **DK Images**: *Steve Tanner cAr;* **Ingram Image Library**: *tcr; p66/67* **Alamy**: *Arcaid tl;* **Alamy RF**: *Ingram Publishing cAr;* **DK Images**: *tr; Stephen Whitehorn bl;* **Ingram Image Library**: *br; p68/69* **Alamy**: *Balearic Pictures cr; directphoto.org cAr; Doug Houghton cl; Indiapicture clB;* **Alamy RF**: *CoverSpot cBl;* **Lee Riches**: *cBr; p72/73* **Alamy RF**: *imagebroker tcrB; Image Source cAr; Comstock Images tcr;* **Avery Weight-Tronix**: *bl; p74/75* **Alamy RF**: *Doug Norman bl;* **Ingram Image Library**: *c; p76/77* **Alamy**: *Balearic Pictures cBl; Indiapicture bl;* **Alamy RF**: *Coverspot clB; p78/79* **Alamy RF**: *Luca DiCecco bcl; Steve Hamblin bcr; p80/81* **Getty**: *Taxi / Rob Melnychuk bc;* **Ingram Image Library**: *cAr; Xerox UK Ltd: tcr; p82/83* **Alamy**: *wildphotos.com tcr;* **Alamy RF**: *FogStock cAAl; Momentum Creative Group cAl; Shoosh / Up the Res cBl;* **Ingram Image Library**: *cl; p84/85* **Alamy**: *Brand X Pictures cr; f1* **Alamy RF**: *BananaStock bl; Comstock Images c; SuperStock tr;* **Ingram Image Library**: *crB; p86/87* **Alamy RF**: *Luca DiCecco bcl;* **Getty**: *Taxi / Rob Melnychuk tc; p90/91* **Alamy RF**: *Brand X Pictures tcr;* **DK Images**: *cl; Stephen Oliver cr;* **Ingram Image Library**: *cBr; p82/93* **Alamy RF**: *Pixland cr;* **DK Images**: *cl; Guy Ryecart tr; p94/95* **Alamy**: *David Kamm cl; Phototake Inc bcl;* **Alamy RF**: *Comstock Images cr; ImageState Royalty Free bcr;* **DK Images**: *Stephen Oliver tcr; p96/97* **Alamy RF**: *Pixland br;* **DK Images**: *tl;* **Ingram Image Library**: *tr; p98/99* **Alamy**: *Andrew Linscott c; Shotfile cr;* **Alamy RF**: *Bildagentur Franz Waldhaeusl bl; ThinkStock br; p100/101* **DK Images**: *Steve Gorton tcr; p102/103* **Alamy**: *Hortus b; D Hurst tcrB;* **Alamy RF**: *image100 tr; p104/105* **DK Images**: *cAr; p104/105* **DK Images**: *Paul Bricknell cl(6); Jane Burton bcl; Geoff Dann cl(2); Max Gibbs cl(4); Frank Greenaway cl(3); Dave King cl(1), cAr, Tracy Morgan c(5); p106/107* **Alamy**: *Shotfile cr;* **Alamy RF**: *Barry Mason br; p110/111* **Alamy RF**: *Think Stock cr;* **DK Images**: *Andy Crawford cl; p112/113* **Alamy RF**: *Dynamic Graphics Group / Creatas tcr; image100 bl;* **Ingram Image Library**: *cl; bcrA; p114/115* **Alamy**: *John Cole cr;* **Alamy RF**: *Image Source cAr; Index Stock cAl; jackhollingsworth.com tcr; p116/117* **Alamy RF**: *Dynamics Graphics Group / Creatas clA; John Foxx clB; p118/119* **Alamy**: *D Hurst c;* **Alamy RF**: *Pixland tcr; p120/121* **Alamy**: *ImageState / Pictor International cl; Shotfile cBl;* **Alamy RF**: *Sarkis Images tcr;* **DK Images**: *bcl; p122/123* **Alamy RF**: *BananaStock cA;* **Ingram Image Library**: *cl; p124/125* **Alamy**: *ImageState / Pictor International bclA; Shotfile cBl;* **DK Images**: *bcl; Paul Bricknell tc(5); Geoff Dann tc(3); Max Gibbs tc(1); Frank Greenaway tc(2); Dave King tc(4); Tracy Morgan tc(6);* **Ingram Image Library**: *bl; p126/127* **Alamy**: *Jean Dominique Dallet clB;* **Alamy RF**: *Imageshop - Zefa Visual Media blA; Image Farm Inc bl; p128* **DK Images**. *All other images* **Mike Good**.